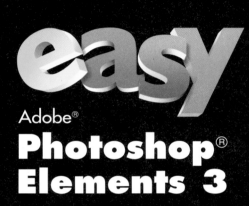

Adobe®
Photoshop®
Elements 3

Contents

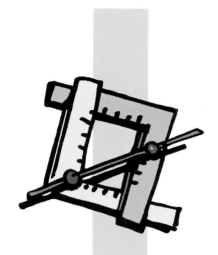

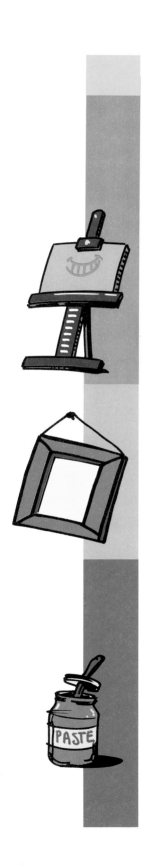

Easy Adobe® Photoshop® Elements 3
Copyright © 2005 by Que Publishing

International Standard Book Number: 0-7897-3330-7

Library of Congress Catalog Card Number: 2004114190

Printed in the United States of America

First Printing: October 2004

07   06   05   04   4   3   2   1

Trademarks
All terms mentioned in this book that are known to be trademarks or service marks have been appropriately capitalized. Que Publishing cannot attest to the accuracy of this information. Use of a term in this book should not be regarded as affecting the validity of any trademark or service mark.

Adobe and Photoshop are registered trademarks of Adobe Systems, Inc.

Warning and Disclaimer

Bulk Sales
Que Publishing offers excellent discounts on this book when ordered in quantity for bulk purchases or special sales. For more information, please contact

U.S. Corporate and Government Sales

1-800-382-3419

corpsales@pearsontechgroup.com

For sales outside of the United States, please contact

International Sales

international@pearsoned.com

Publisher
Paul Boger

Associate Publisher
Greg Wiegand

Acquisitions Editor
Michelle Newcomb

Development Editor
Laura Norman

Managing Editor
Charlotte Clapp

Project Editor
Dan Knott

Indexer
Ken Johnson

Technical Editor
Lisa Lee

Publishing Coordinator
Sharry Lee Gregory

Book Designer
Anne Jones

Page Layout
Michelle Mitchell

About the Author

Kate Binder is a design and graphics expert who works from her home in New Hampshire. She has written articles on graphics, publishing, and photography for magazines including *Shutterbug*, *Publish*, *eDigital Photo*, *PEI*, and *Desktop Publishers Journal*. Kate is also the author of several books, including *Easy Mac OS X v10.3 Panther*, *The Complete Idiot's Guide to Mac OS X*, and *Easy Adobe Photoshop 6*, and she is the coauthor of books including *Microsoft Office: Mac v.X Inside Out*, *Easy Mac OS X*, *The Complete Idiot's Guide to Mac OS X*, *SVG for Designers*, and *Get Creative: The Digital Photo Idea Book*.

Kate's website is **http://www.prospecthillpub.com**.

Dedication

To Big Patrick and Little Patrick, both of whom keep me going on hard days.

Acknowledgments

My thanks go first to my family, as always: my husband and partner Don, who makes me lunch every day; our son Mack, who amazes me every day; and my parents Richard and Barbara, without whom…well, that's pretty obvious. And thank you once more to Laura Norman and Michelle Newcomb at Que, for walking me through another one. The rest of the gang at Que deserves kudos, too, especially project editor Dan Knott, production editor Megan Wade, and technical editor Lisa Lee.

Many of the models for the photos in this book are retired racing greyhounds—a most extraordinary breed of dog. To learn more about how greyhounds make wonderful pets, visit **www.adopt-a-greyhound.org**.

—Kate Binder

We Want to Hear from You!

As the reader of this book, *you* are our most important critic and commentator. We value your opinion and want to know what we're doing right, what we could do better, what areas you'd like to see us publish in, and any other words of wisdom you're willing to pass our way.

As an associate publisher for Que Publishing, I welcome your comments. You can email or write me directly to let me know what you did or didn't like about this book—as well as what we can do to make our books better.

Please note that I cannot help you with technical problems related to the topic of this book. We do have a User Services group, however, where I will forward specific technical questions related to the book.

When you write, please be sure to include this book's title and author as well as your name, email address, and phone number. I will carefully review your comments and share them with the author and editors who worked on the book.

Email: **feedback@quepublishing.com**

Mail: Greg Wiegand
            Associate Publisher
            Que Publishing
            800 East 96th Street
            Indianapolis, IN 46240 USA

For more information about this book or another Que Publishing title, visit our website at **www.quepublishing.com**. Type the ISBN (excluding hyphens) or the title of a book in the Search field to find the page you're looking for.

It's as Easy as 1-2-3

Each part of this book is made up of a series of short, instructional lessons, designed to help you understand basic information that you need to get the most out of your computer hardware and software.

Each step is fully illustrated to show you how it looks onscreen.

2 Each task includes a series of quick, easy steps designed to guide you through the procedure.

3 Items that you select or click in menus, dialog boxes, tabs, and windows are shown in **bold**.

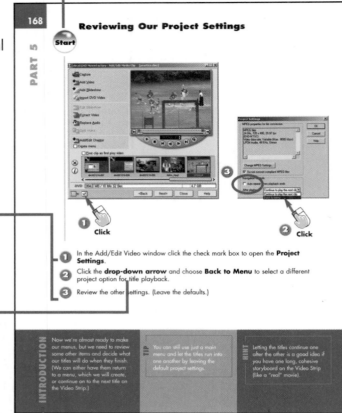

PART 5

Start

Click   **Click**

1 In the Add/Edit Video window click the check mark box to open the **Project Settings**.

2 Click the **drop-down arrow** and choose **Back to Menu** to select a different project option for title playback.

3 Review the other settings. (Leave the defaults.)

INTRODUCTION   Now we're almost ready to make our menus, but we need to review some other items and decide what our titles will do when they finish. (We can either have them return to a menu, which we will create, or continue on to the next title on the Video Strip.)

TIP   You can still use just a main menu and let the titles run into one another by leaving the default project settings.

HINT   Letting the titles continue one after the other is a good idea if you have one long, cohesive storyboard on the Video Strip (like a "real" movie).

drag

drop

How to Drag:
Point to the starting place or object. Hold down the mouse button (right or left per instructions), move the mouse to the new location, then release the button.

See next page

End

Introductions explain what you will learn in each task, and **Tips and Hints** give you a heads-up for any extra information you may need while working through the task

See next page:
If you see this symbol, it means the task you're working on continues on the next page.

End Task:
Task is complete.

Selection:
Highlights the area onscreen discussed in the step or task.

Click:
Click the left mouse button once.

Double-click:
Click the left mouse button twice in rapid succession.

Right-click:
Click the right mouse button once.

Pointer Arrow:
Highlights an item on the screen you need to point to or focus on in the step or task.

Click & Type:
Click once where indicated and begin typing to enter your text or data.

Introduction to Easy Adobe Photoshop Elements

This is a book for people who dislike computer books—even for people who might not be particularly fond of computers or adept at using them.

You might simply love your digital camera or just love the ease of sharing photos electronically with a few special people on the planet who really care about what's going on in your life.

And certainly you have to love the ability to store thousands of pictures on your computer's hard drive, and perhaps thousands more on CDs you burn. Gone are the shoeboxes full of curling, faded prints that are still waiting for the happy day when you will have so much time on your hands you'll finally get around to sorting them, labeling them, and pasting them neatly into leather-covered albums.

What's that you say? The shoeboxes are still there?

Don't you own a scanner? Now those prints of yesteryear simply await the happy day when you'll finally get around to sorting them, scanning them....

Let's face it: One thing you don't have is a lot of time.

And if you did find some time, you'd pick up a real book by Elizabeth Peters or Tom Clancy, kick back, and enjoy yourself.

Who wants to read about computers?

Not me, that's for sure. I'm a lot like you. I love my digital camera. I look forward to sharing my pictures, but I don't want to spend hours "playing" with them. I spend enough time sitting at a computer when I'm working—when it comes to my family photos, vacation snapshots, and eBay listing photos, I just want to get them looking good as quickly as possible so I can get on with my life.

And that's exactly where Photoshop Elements fits into my plans. Now, I spend a lot of hours using Big Photoshop in my work. And I love the program, I really do. But, as I said earlier, I don't feel like getting out the big guns after hours. But I'm used to the power of Photoshop—after all, it's the industry-standard image editor, and there's just not much it can't do. Given that, is it really possible for Photoshop Elements to keep me happy?

The answer, it turns out, is emphatically yes. With Photoshop Elements, you get maximum results with minimum effort. And version 3 offers more of the same, only better, with a special editing mode (Quick Fix) that hides all the tools and options you don't need and makes it even easier to use the ones you do. Retouching doesn't get much easier than the new Healing Brush tool. And built-in wizards do all the heavy lifting involved in creating everything from photo album pages and greeting cards to wall calendars and web galleries.

So, here's hoping that you love Photoshop Elements as much as I do—and that this book enables you to use the program to create images you'll love even more.

May you enjoy this book, thrill as I did at the tricks you can do with Photoshop Elements, and not spend a minute more than you need to with either of them.

Learning the Ropes

Back when ships needed favorable winds to get anywhere, new recruits had to learn which ropes to pull to carry out the captain's orders and set sail. This first part of the book is for novice sailors—people who feel more comfortable if they can begin at the beginning, while their ship is still safely docked. Just turn the page to sign on for a brief orientation session: You'll quickly learn the commands, controls, and features of the Photoshop Elements work area. For example, you'll find out what a *tool* is and how to select one from the *toolbox*. After you have your bearings, we can shorthand the steps in later parts and just say, "Click the **Crop** tool," and move on.

If you're feeling adventurous, don't worry about sailing ahead to another part of the book. You can do most of the tasks in any order, and you can always come back to this part if somehow you get turned around.

Welcome aboard, and fear not: You have nothing to lose but your old film cameras and the tiresome wait for your prints to come back from the lab.

The Photoshop Elements Work Area

Title bar

Search (for help) field

Menu bar

Shortcuts bar

Options bar

Toolbox

Palettes

Palette Bin

Photo Bin

Active image area

Starting Photoshop Elements and Opening a Picture

Start

Double-click

Click

1 Double-click the **Adobe Photoshop Elements 3.0** icon on the Windows Desktop to start the program.

2 Click the **Edit and Enhance Photos** button or the **Quickly Fix Photos** button to work on an existing photo.

Photoshop Elements has two working modes: Quick Fix mode, for making instant automated image corrections, and Standard Edit mode, for more complex operations. To use either, you first have to start Elements and open your image.

TIP

Welcome Back
Click the arrow next to **Start Up in** to choose a different startup option. You can have Elements open the Editor or Organizer rather than showing the Welcome screen. If you want it back, select **Window**, **Welcome** from the menu bar.

Click ③

Click ⑤   **Click** ④

Click ⑥

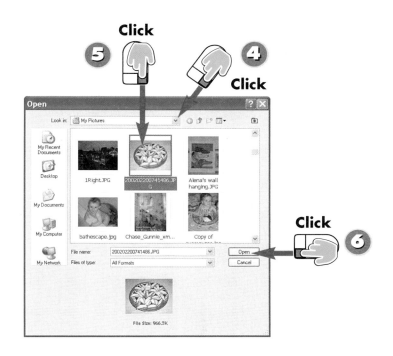

③ Select **File**, **Open** from the menu bar.

④ Navigate to the folder where your image files are stored.

⑤ Click the file you want to open.

⑥ Click the **Open** button. The picture opens in the active image area.

End

Hide and Seek

Don't see your shots? Either you didn't load them from your camera or scanner yet or you stored them in a different folder. You might need to navigate the filesystem on your hard drive or CD to find the images you want. Turn to the next task, "Browsing for a File," to learn how.

Browsing for a File

Start

Click

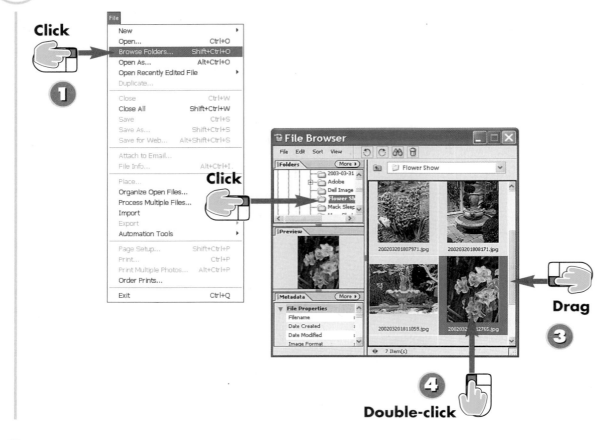

Click

Drag

3

4

Double-click

① To look for a file, select **File**, **Browse Folders** from the menu bar.

② Click the folder name that contains the picture files you want.

③ Drag the **scrollbar** to browse the picture files in the folder.

④ Double-click the thumbnail view of the file you want. It opens in the active image area, ready for editing.

 End

INTRODUCTION

If you remember the photo you want to open but don't remember its name, use Elements's File Browser to view thumbnails of each photo in a folder, accompanied by metadata about those images, such as the time and date they were created.

HINT

Exploring Files
The directory of file folders in the upper-left corner of the File Browser window works just like Windows Explorer.

HINT

Managing Images
Elements's Organizer mode is like the File Browser on steroids—you can use it to sort and search your image collection in a flash. Turn to Part 8, "Building Albums and Presentations," **p.144**, to learn more about Organizer.

Starting Photoshop Elements with a Blank Canvas

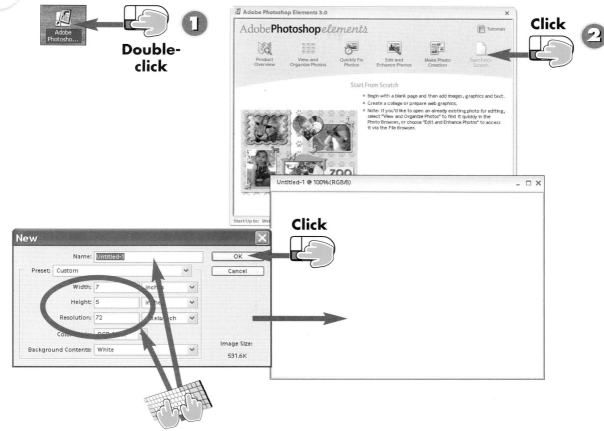

Double-click

Click

Click

① Double-click the **Adobe Photoshop Elements 3.0** icon on the Windows Desktop to start the program.

② Click the **Start from Scratch** button to create a new, blank image file.

③ Enter **Width**, **Height**, and **Resolution** values and give the new file a name.

④ Click **OK** to create the new file. A blank image window opens.

End

INTRODUCTION

Not all images start out as photographs. Sometimes, you just want to paint. For that to happen, you need to start with a blank document, rather than opening an existing file. You can choose the size and resolution of your new image file.

HINT

The Color of the Canvas
You can choose your background from the Background Contents drop-down menu. White gives you a blank white "page" to draw on, and Background Color makes the canvas whatever color is the current background color.

TIP

Sizing for a Copied Image
If an image is on the clipboard, Photoshop Elements automatically inserts the size and resolution of that image in the New dialog box. Click **OK**; then press **Ctrl+V** to paste the image into the document.

Viewing and Adjusting the Active Image Area

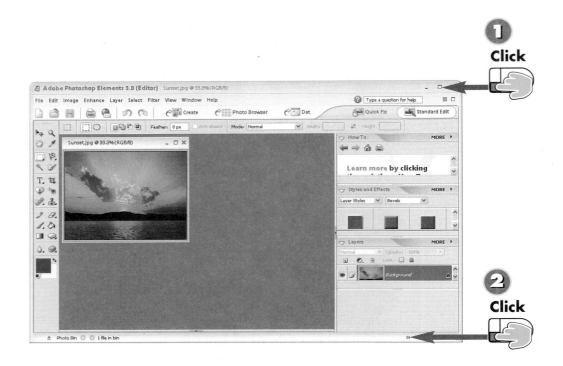

1 Click

2 Click

1 Click the program window's **Maximize** button so that the Elements window fills the entire screen.

2 To clear the work area, click the arrow to close the Palette Bin.

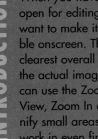

When you have a picture file open for editing, you'll usually want to make it as large as possible onscreen. This gives you the clearest overall view, regardless of the actual image size. Then, you can use the Zoom tool (or the View, Zoom In command) to magnify small areas if you need to work in even finer detail.

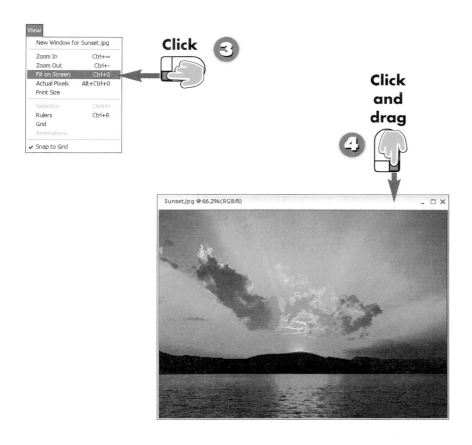

Click

Click and drag

From the menu bar, select **View**, **Fit on Screen** or press **Ctrl+0** (zero). The active image window enlarges to fill the work area.

Click and drag the active image window's title bar to move the window around.

End

Selecting Tools from the Toolbox

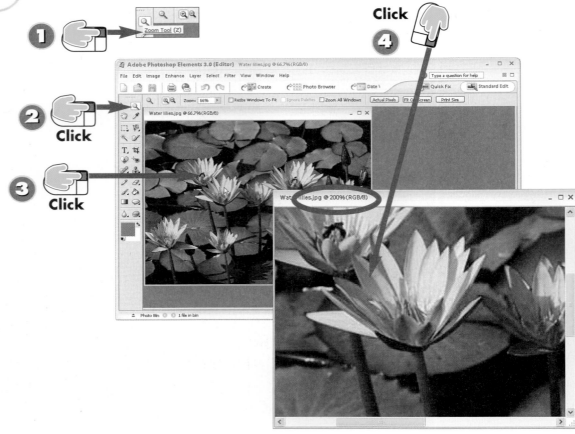

Start

1. Hover and pause the pointer over the **Zoom** tool. Its name appears in a ScreenTip, along with the letter of its shortcut key.

2. Click the **Zoom** tool or press **Z**. The pointer changes to a magnifying-glass symbol, and settings that affect the tool appear in the options bar.

3. Move the pointer to the center of the area you want enlarged, and click. A magnified view appears in the active image area.

4. Click again and again to enlarge the view in progressive steps. The magnification percentage appears in the title bar.

INTRODUCTION

Tools in the toolbox help you work on portions of a picture in a variety of ways. An example is the Zoom tool, which enlarges your view of a picture. You can select the Zoom tool by clicking it in the toolbox or by pressing Z on the keyboard.

HINT

Zoom In
Zooming doesn't make any changes to the picture itself, just to your view of it in Photoshop Elements so you can work on fine details.

TIP

Shortcut
When using the Zoom tool, right-click anywhere within the active image area and select **Fit on Screen** to quickly view the entire image.

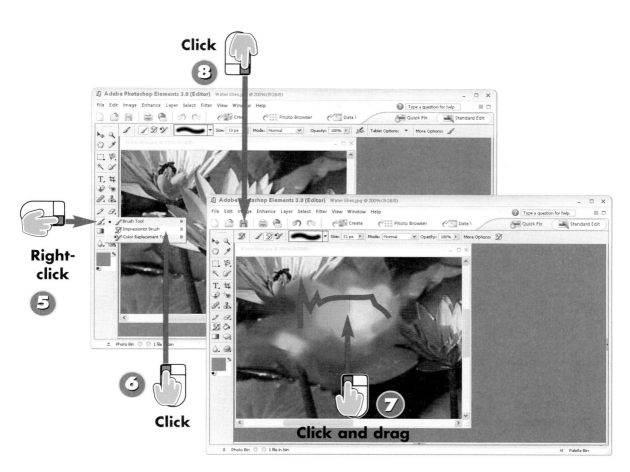

Click

Right-click

Click

Click and drag

5 Right-click the **Brush** tool.

6 Select the **Impressionist Brush** tool. The pointer changes to the brush tip, and settings for the tool appear in the options bar.

7 Move the pointer to the area of the picture where you want to use the brush; then click and drag it around, as if painting, to apply the effect.

8 Because you made a change to the picture, click the **Save** shortcut in the Shortcuts bar to save your work.

End

Best-Quality Image
After you've made changes to a JPEG file, for best quality, you should use the File, Save As command to convert it to TIFF (**.tif**) format or save it as a Photoshop (**.psd**) file.

It's All a Blur
For other ways to get softened or blurred effects, try the Smudge or Blur tools, or one of the various Blur commands from the Filter menu.

First Impressions
You can vary the effect of the Impressionist Brush by changing settings in the options bar—Brush Size, Blending Mode, and Opacity, to name a few. To admire the overall result of your brushwork, select **View, Fit on Screen** from the menu bar.

Controlling How Tools Behave with the Options Bar

Start

Click ① **Click** ②

Click ③

Click ④

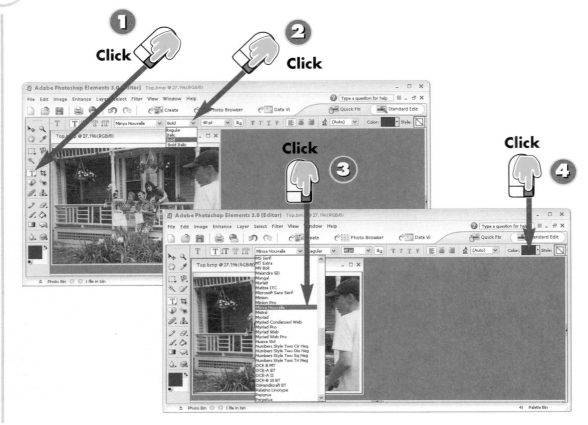

① In the toolbox, click the **Horizontal Type** tool, or press **T**. Settings for the tool appear in the options bar.

② Select a **Font Style** and **Font Size** from the drop-down menus in the options bar.

③ Use the **Font** drop-down menu to select a new font for your text, such as **Minya Nouvelle**.

④ Click the **Text Color** box; the Color Picker window opens.

After you select a tool from the toolbox, you can change settings in the options bar that control its effect. Try it with the Horizontal Type tool.

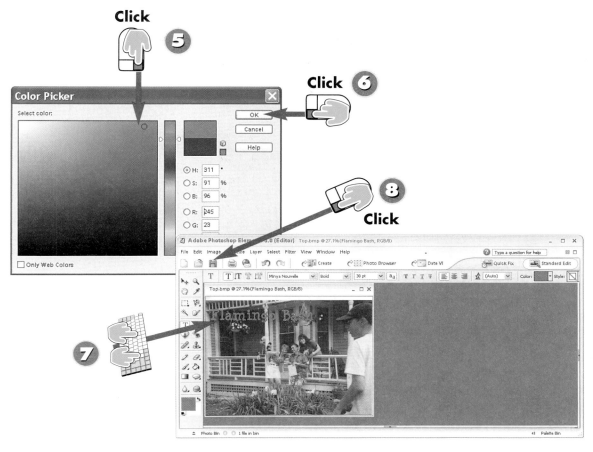

5 In the Color Picker, click the upper-left corner of the color space to select **Magenta**.

6 Click **OK**.

7 Type some text, such as **Flamingo Bash**.

8 Click the **Save** shortcut to save your work.

End

HINT

Settings Retained
Settings you make in the options bar remain in effect for a particular tool until you change them again, even if you quit and then restart the program.

Using Palettes

Start

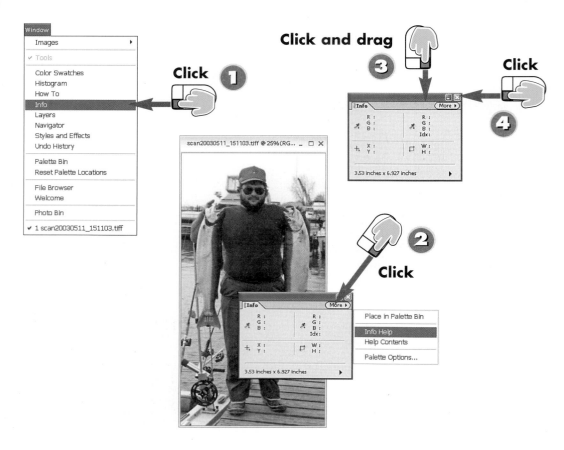

Click ①

Click and drag ③

Click ④

Click ②

① In Standard Edit mode, select a palette name, such as **Info**, from the **Window** menu to open a palette.

② Click the palette's **More** button to see a menu of commands related to the palette's function.

③ Drag the palette's title bar to move it around the screen.

④ Click the palette's close box to dismiss the palette.

End

INTRODUCTION

Palettes, floating windows that contain help and commands grouped by category, are a truly handy feature. For example, the Info palette shows color values and measurements for the current image or selected area.

HINT

Getting More
The selections in the More menu are different for each palette.

TIP

Layer Info
Especially as you begin to combine images or create artwork from them, get in the habit of leaving the Layers palette open. As you add text, graphics, painting, or images, you'll quickly see why keeping track of layers is important.

Using the Palette Bin

Start

Click ②

Drag ③

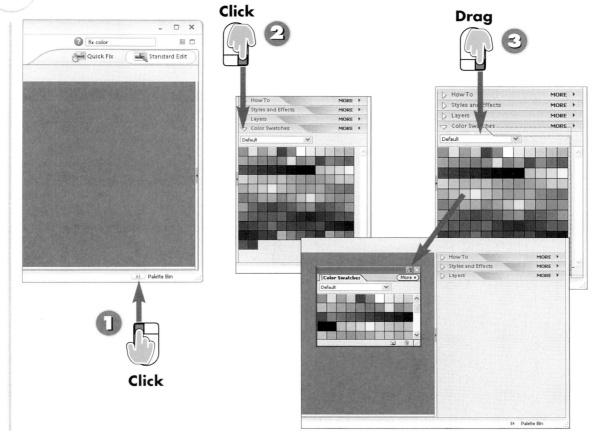

Click ①

Click

① In Standard Edit mode, click the arrow labeled **Palette Bin** to open the bin.

② Click the disclosure triangle in the title bar of a palette in the Palette Bin to expand or shrink the palette.

③ Drag a palette's title bar to remove it from the Palette Bin.

End

INTRODUCTION

Floating palettes are great, but they take up a lot of space on your screen. The Palette Bin on the right side of your screen is a handy place to stash palettes so they don't obscure your view of the image you're working on.

HINT

Viewing Palettes
To use the Palette Bin effectively, set your screen resolution to at least 1024 × 768. If you work at 640 × 480 or 800 × 600, you'll run out of room to expand palettes in the bin. It is easier to select them individually from the Windows menu.

TIP

Adding to the Bin
To replace a palette in the Palette Bin, make sure a check mark is next to the Place in Palette Bin option in the palette's More menu; then click its close button.

Using Contextual Menus

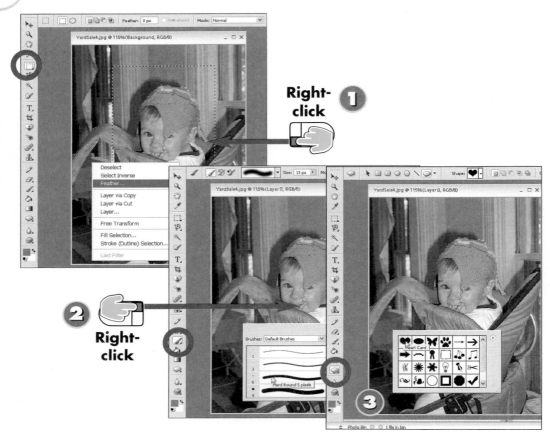

Right-click ①

Right-click ②

① With a selection tool active, right-click in the image area to see a menu of selection commands.

② With a painting tool active, right-click in the image area to see a menu of brush shapes.

③ With a shape tool active, right-click in the image area to see a menu of drawing shapes.

End

INTRODUCTION

Contextual menus pop up at the tip of your mouse cursor when you right-click in the image window. They're contextual because their contents change depending on which tool you're using, so the commands are always appropriate to their context.

HINT

Keeping Things in Context
Be sure to try right-clicking with each tool to see all the contextual menus Photoshop Elements has to offer. Using them is a real time-saver.

TIP

Layer by Layer
When you're building layered images (see Part 9, "Using Layers to Combine Photos and Artwork," **p.158**, to learn more), you can quickly switch layers by right-clicking with the Move tool or a selection tool.

Switching Between Quick Fix and Standard Edit Modes

Start

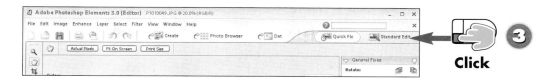
Click **3**

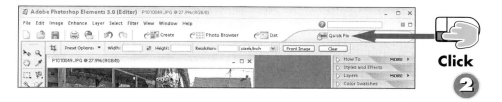
Click **2**

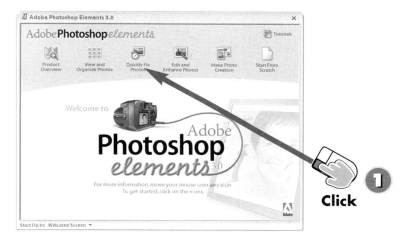

Click **1**

1 Click the **Quickly Fix Photos** button on the welcome screen to get to Quick Fix mode, or click the **Edit and Enhance Photos** button to open in Standard Edit mode.

2 When you're in Standard Edit mode, click the **Quick Fix** button to switch to Quick Fix mode.

3 When you're in Quick Fix mode, click the **Standard Edit** button to switch to Standard Edit mode.

End

Photoshop Elements has two working modes. In Standard Edit mode, all of Photoshop Elements's tools and palettes are available to you. In Quick Fix mode, the program's interface is stripped down to just the controls you need to apply fast, automated edits.

TIP

Fixing It Quickly
You can still make quick fixes when you're in Standard Edit mode. You can use the Auto commands in the Enhance menu to adjust color, lighting, and contrast (or use Enhance, Auto Smart Fix to adjust everything at once).

Following a Recipe

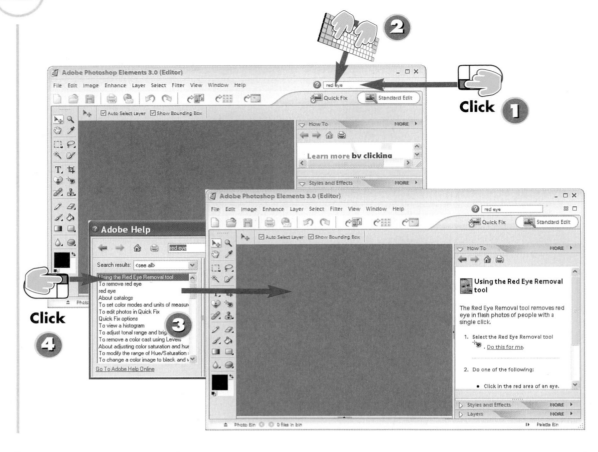

1 Click inside the search box.

2 Type a phrase that describes what you want to do, such as **Red Eye**.

3 Press **Enter**. If the program finds a match, a list of recipes opens.

4 Click the topic that best fits your request. The How To palette opens, showing step-by-step instructions.

End

Photoshop Elements has a lot of ways to give you suggestions when you can't remember the steps you need to take—or even where to begin. Here's one of the easiest: Just type your request and pick a precooked solution.

HINT

Follow the Recipe
Before you can follow the recipe's steps, you must have a picture open in the active image area. Otherwise, you'll know what to do but lose the benefit of being able to apply the advice immediately.

TIP

No Recipes Found?
If the search reports **No Recipes Found** or none do the trick, click the drop-down menu under the **Search Results** tab and select **Results for Help**. A list of related Help topics appears. Click a topic and read its advice.

Taking a Tutorial

Start

Click
1

Click
4

Drag
3

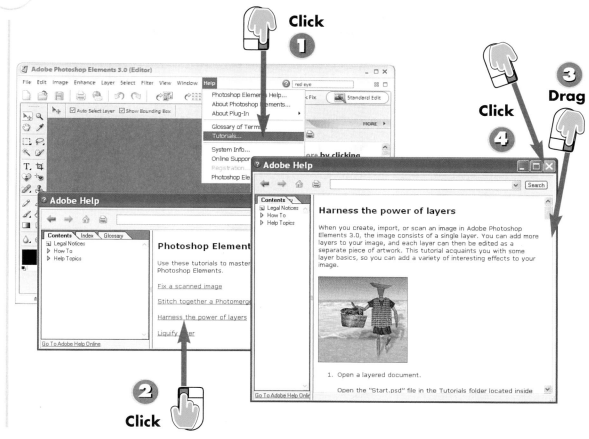

Click
2

1 From the menu bar, select **Help**, **Tutorials**.

2 In the Help window, click the title of the lesson you want.

3 Drag the **scrollbar** to read through the lesson.

4 When you're done, close the Help window to return to the program work area.

End

INTRODUCTION

Photoshop Elements has online lessons for popular tasks that take more than a few steps. Try this built-in advice on fixing a scanned image, stitching together a panorama, working with layers, using the Liquify filter, and more.

TIP

Choose from the Index
If you don't see a lesson on the topic you want, look in the recipes in the How To palette, or select **Help**, **Photoshop Elements Help**. Then, click **Index** and select a topic from the alphabetized list.

Setting Preferences

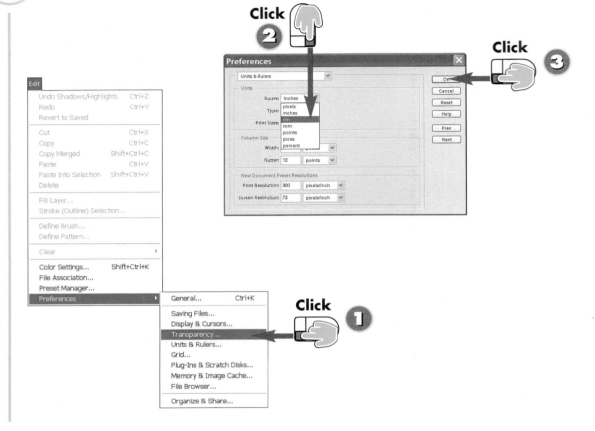

1 From the menu bar, select **Edit**, **Preferences** and choose one of the commands from the submenu.

2 Set the options you want to change. For example, select **cm** in the **Rulers** drop-down menu to change the unit of measure from inches to centimeters

3 Click **OK**.

End

These steps show you where to look if you want to customize how Photoshop Elements shows things in the work area, how it saves files, and other options. As just one of many options, these steps explain how to change the unit of measure in the work area from inches to centimeters.

HINT

Default Settings
Default preference settings work fine for most people. Experiment with the settings as you get more comfortable with the software. You might improve efficiency by changing a preference if you always have to change a setting manually.

TIP

Restore Defaults
To restore default settings, restart the program and, when it's finished loading, press **Alt+Ctrl+Shift** and select **Yes**. The defaults will be restored the next time you start the program.

Saving Your Work

Start

Click
1

2

4
Click

3
Click

1 To save a file to a different drive or folder or with a different name, select **File**, **Save As** from the menu bar or press **Shift+Ctrl+S**.

2 Type a name for the new file, such as **mackpeppy**. (No need to type the extension, such as **.jpg**.)

3 Optionally, make a selection from the **Format** drop-down menu to change the file type.

4 Use the **Save In** drop-down menu to store the file in a different folder or on a different drive. Click **Save**.

End

INTRODUCTION

All the work you do on a picture in Photoshop Elements will be lost unless you save the file to disk. If you are saving a file for the first time, you can simply click the **Save** button on the Shortcuts bar or press **Ctrl+S** on the keyboard. If you need to save a file to another location or under a new name, these steps show you how.

HINT

File Types
You can keep digital snapshots in the format the camera makes, usually JPEG (**.jpg**) files. But if you want more flexibility in editing them later and the best image quality, it's better to save them as Photoshop (**.psd**) files.

HINT

Digital Negatives
If your computer can burn CDs, save your unedited camera originals to discs. These are your digital "negatives." That way, if you make changes to an image on your hard drive, you still have a copy of the untouched original.

Getting It All Together

In this part, you'll learn how to bring pictures into your computer so you can work with them in Photoshop Elements.

First, you can't do much of anything with your pictures until they exist as digital files on your computer's hard drive. Photos you take with your digital camera, DV camcorder, or camera phone are already stored as files, but you'll need to transfer them from the camera's internal storage to a disk in the computer.

You can also work with film shots—prints, negatives, and slides—but you'll have to *digitize* them first. That's what a scanner does. It scans a print with a beam of light, breaking the image into a collection of individual colored dots, or *pixels* (picture elements). All digital images are composed of pixels, and the main thing Photoshop Elements does is help you change the colors of thousands or even millions of pixels at once, in interesting and useful ways.

You can also grab pictures from other computer documents and from Web pages on the Internet.

Whether you use the other tasks in this book to work with your shots a little or a lot, you'll also learn how to create finished images as prints, contact sheets, and digital photo archives.

The Ins and Outs of Digital Photography

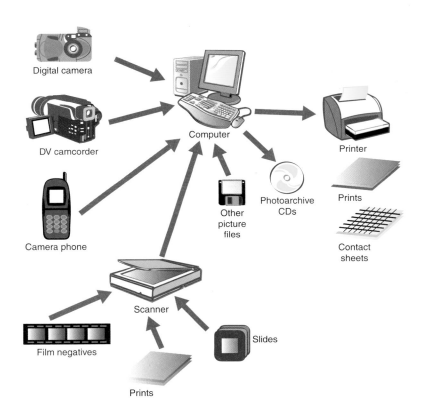

Getting Photos into Your Computer

Start

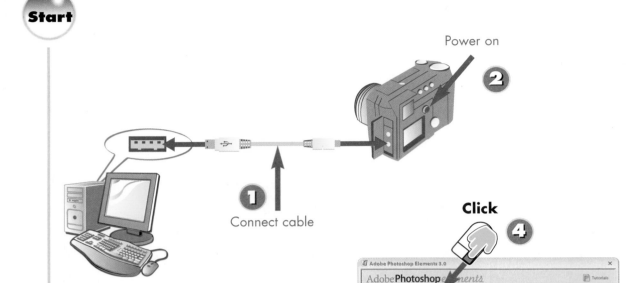

Power on ②

Connect cable ①

Click ④

Double-click ③

① Connect the smaller end of the data cable to the camera, and the larger end to the USB port of your PC.

② Turn the camera power on.

③ Double-click the program icon on the Windows Desktop to start Photoshop Elements.

④ In the Welcome screen, click **View and Organize Photos**.

INTRODUCTION

Most digital cameras and camera phones come with their own software for browsing image files and uploading them to your computer. However, you can use the steps described here to transfer files from most digital picture devices using the built-in functions of Photoshop Elements.

TIP

Getting There from Here
If you're already working in Photoshop Elements when you want to import photos, click the **Photo Browser** button in the Editor's shortcuts bar.

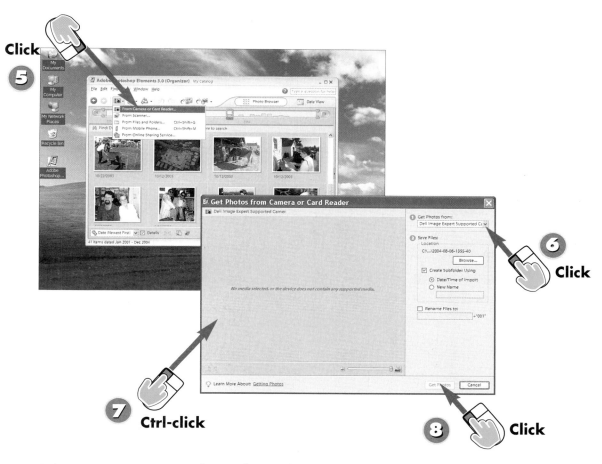

Click **5**

Click **6**

Ctrl-click **7**

Click **8**

5 Select **Camera or Card Reader** in the **Get Photos from** menu in the Shortcuts bar.

6 Choose your camera from the pop-up menu.

7 **Ctrl**-click to select the photos you want to import.

8 Click **Get Photos**.

End

What's in a Name?
Photoshop Elements automatically puts your images into a folder it names with the current date and time. You can specify a different name for the folder by clicking New Name and typing the name you want to use.

Let Me See Your ID
If you like to use filenames to identify photos (such as when you're printing contact sheets), check the **Rename Files to** box and type a word or two in the text entry field. Elements renames the images with that text, plus a sequential number.

Alphabet Soup
Cameras generate filenames automatically, depending on the make and model. For example: **Pmdd0000.jpg**, where **P** = still photo, **m** = single-digit month (1–9, A–C), **dd** = two-digit day, and an **image number** (0001–9999).

Scanning Images

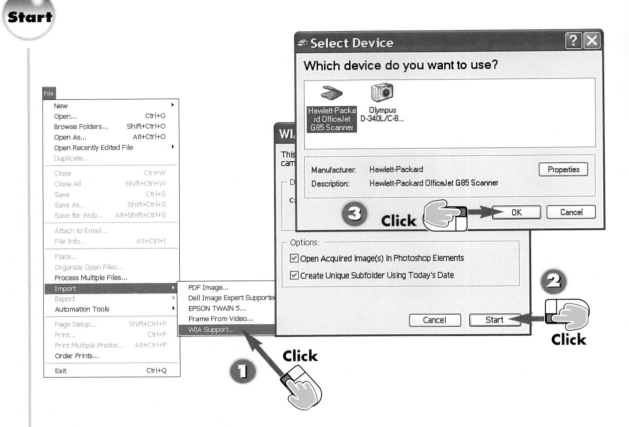

1. With the item to be scanned on the scanner glass and the lid closed, open Photoshop Elements and choose **File**, **Import**, **WIA Support**.

2. Click **Start**.

3. If you have more than one camera or scanner attached to your computer, select the scanning device you want to use, and click **OK**.

Final Destination
These steps create a file automatically. Specify the disk location in the Destination Folder field of the WIA Support dialog box. Be sure to resave the file if you edit the image.

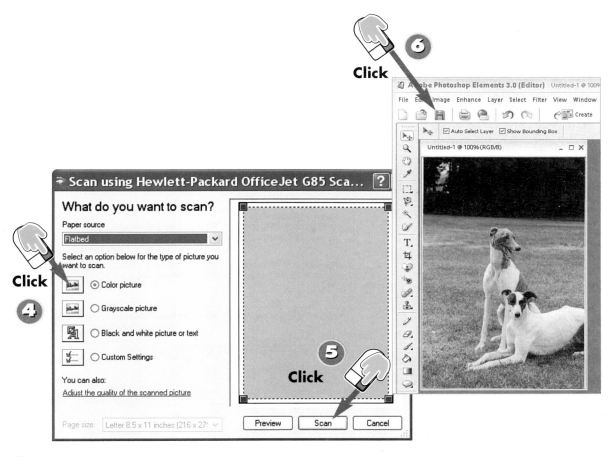

Click 6

Click 4

Click 5

4 Select the type of picture, such as **Color Picture**.

5 Click **Scan**. The scanned print appears in the active image area, ready for editing.

6 After you edit the picture, click the **Save** button to save your work.

End

Not My Type
The WIA (Windows Image Acquisition) Support feature scans a photo as a Windows bitmap (**.bmp** extension) by default. To change the file type, select **File**, **Save As** and change the **Format** after the image has been imported.

Scanning Secrets
The dialog box in step 5 might look different, depending on your scanner model. When adjusting quality, you can select grayscale instead of black and white to capture shading. Use color instead of grayscale if a monochrome picture is sepia. For photos you might want to print later, set the resolution to 300 dpi.

Grabbing a Video Frame

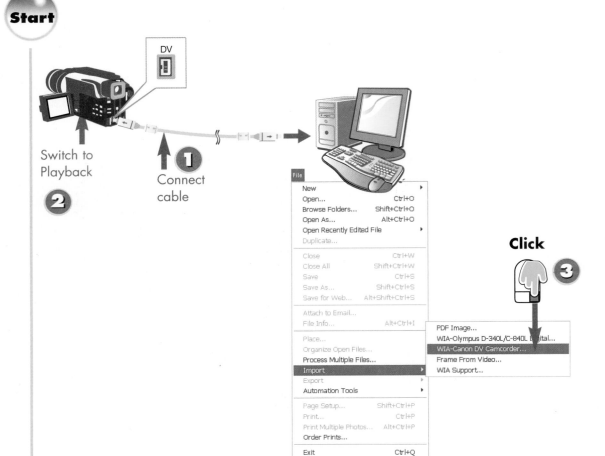

Switch to Playback ②

Connect cable ①

Click ③

① Connect the smaller end of the data cable to the camcorder, and the larger end to the FireWire port of your PC.

② Switch the camcorder to **Playback** (or VCR) mode.

③ From the Photoshop Elements menu bar, select **File**, **Import**, **WIA** *<camera name>*. Press **Play** on the camcorder to roll the tape.

Photoshop Elements can't capture still photos from uploaded DV files (**.mov** extension), but you can follow these steps to capture one or more stills as the camcorder plays back a tape, which achieves the same result.

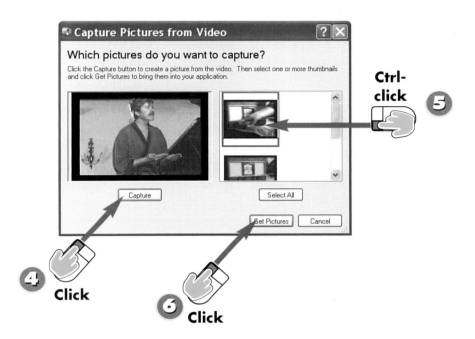

Ctrl-
click **5**

4 Click

6 Click

4 Video plays in the screen on the left. When you see the frame you want, click **Capture**. (Repeat if you want multiple frames.)

5 Press **Ctrl** while you click each thumbnail you want (or click **Select All** to get all of them).

6 Click **Get Pictures**. The video stills open for editing in separate windows in the work area.

End

Video Capture
To capture video files you already have on disk that are in a format other than **.mov**, turn the page and follow the steps in "Capturing a Frame from a Video File."

Other Options
For these steps to work with your camcorder, it must be a WIA device. If you have an older DV camcorder, upload the clips as **.mov** files, use a video editor such as Pinnacle Studio to save as a Windows movie (**.wmv**), and then select the **File, Import, Frame from Video** command instead.

Capturing a Frame from a Video File

Start

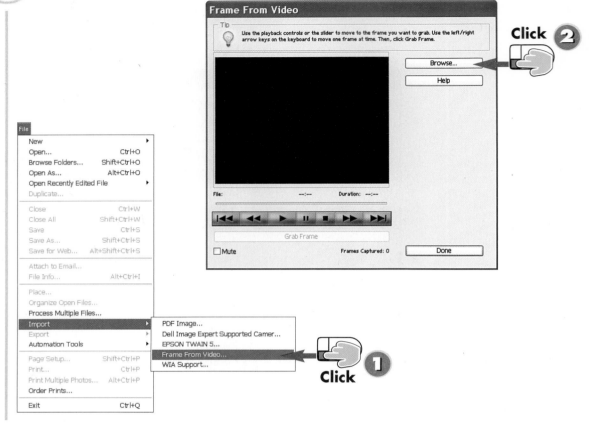

Frame From Video

Tip
Use the playback controls or the slider to move to the frame you want to grab. Use the left/right arrow keys on the keyboard to move one frame at time. Then, click Grab Frame.

Browse...

Help

File: --:--   Duration: --:--

Grab Frame

☐ Mute   Frames Captured: 0   Done

Click 2

File

New ▸	
Open...	Ctrl+O
Browse Folders...	Shift+Ctrl+O
Open As...	Alt+Ctrl+O
Open Recently Edited File ▸	
Duplicate...	
Close	Ctrl+W
Close All	Shift+Ctrl+W
Save	Ctrl+S
Save As...	Shift+Ctrl+S
Save for Web...	Alt+Shift+Ctrl+S
Attach to Email...	
File Info...	Alt+Ctrl+I
Place...	
Organize Open Files...	
Process Multiple Files...	
Import ▸	
Export ▸	
Automation Tools ▸	
Page Setup...	Shift+Ctrl+P
Print...	Ctrl+P
Print Multiple Photos...	Alt+Ctrl+P
Order Prints...	
Exit	Ctrl+Q

PDF Image...
Dell Image Expert Supported Camer...
EPSON TWAIN 5...
Frame From Video...
WIA Support...

Click 1

1 From the menu bar, select **File**, **Import**, **Frame from Video**.

2 Click **Browse** to locate the video file to use.

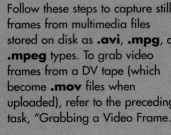

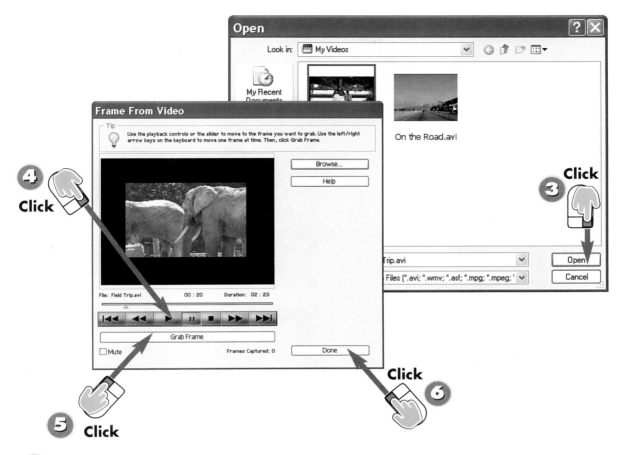

3 Select the file and click **Open**.

4 The video clip opens in the preview pane. Click the **Play** button to start playing it.

5 When you see the frame you want, click **Grab Frame** or press the **spacebar**. (Repeat if you want multiple frames.)

6 Click **Done**. The frames you selected will open in the work area for editing.

Grab It

For more accuracy in grabbing the exact frame you want in step 5, click the **Pause** button to freeze playback. You can press the **right** and **left arrow** keys to move forward or backward a frame at a time.

Unwind a Little

If the Rewind and Fast Forward buttons are grayed out, the type of clip you've selected doesn't support rewinding or fast-forwarding.

Taking an Image from the Clipboard

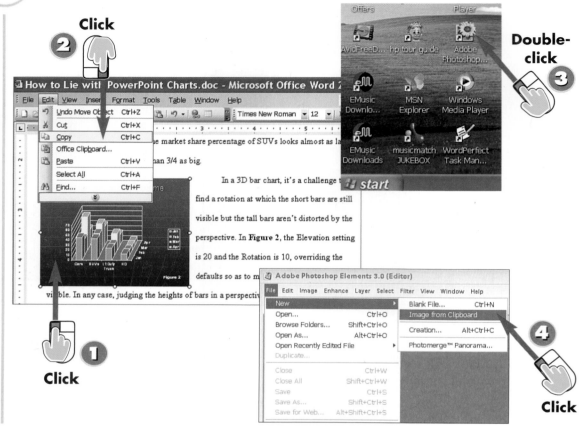

Click ②

Double-click ③

Click ①

Click ④

① In another Windows application, such as Microsoft Word, click the image you want.

② From the application's menu bar, select **Edit**, **Copy** or press **Ctrl+C**.

③ Start Photoshop Elements (or click its button on the Windows taskbar if it's already open).

④ From the Photoshop Elements menu bar, select **File**, **Image from Clipboard**. A copy of the picture opens in the active image window for editing.

End

Native Files

HINT

The copied image comes into Photoshop Elements in whatever format it was in the original document, but if you edit it and then try to save, the program will prompt you to save it as a native Photoshop (**.psd**) file. Saving a copy of your image as a **.psd** file is a good idea, as it enables you to continue making edits to the file. If you save as another format, such as **.jpg** or **.gif**, the changes you make are incorporated into the file, and you can no longer undo them.

Copying a Picture from a Web Page

Start

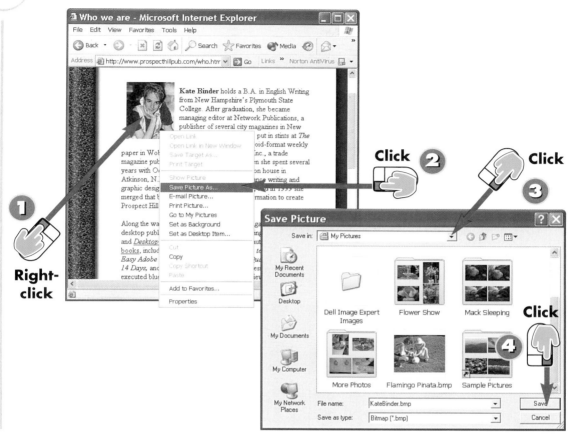

Click ② **Click** ③

Right-click ①

Click ④

1. While viewing a Web page in Internet Explorer (or other browser), right-click the picture you want.

2. From the pop-up menu, select **Save Picture As** (or the equivalent command in your browser).

3. If necessary, navigate to the folder where you want to store the file.

4. Click **Save**. You're ready to open the file in Photoshop Elements for editing.

End

INTRODUCTION

Think of the Internet as a global photo library at your fingertips. For example, if you need a photo of the Brooklyn Bridge to illustrate a report, surf to **www.google.com**, click the **Images** tab, and you're sure to find several choices. Then use the steps here to load the image into Photoshop Elements.

HINT

Know Your Rights
Photos and artwork on the Web are subject to copyright. Obtain permission from the rights holder before incorporating them in your Web sites, slideshows, or newsletters.

TIP

A New Name
You can type a new name for the file in the **File Name** box before you select **Save**. Don't type the extension part or try to change it.

Scanning a Slide

Start

1 Insert

2 Click

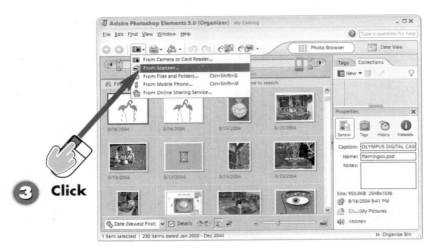

3 Click

1 Insert the slide in the scanner, emulsion (dull) side up. (If your scanner has a backlit transparency attachment, use it.)

2 In Photoshop Elements, click the **Photo Browser** button in the Shortcuts bar.

3 In the Organizer, click the **Get Photos** button and choose **From Scanner** in the drop-down menu. Elements automatically detects your scanner and starts up the scanner software.

You can scan your old slides much as you do prints. Many scanners have special transparency adapters you can buy, which provide backlight for a brighter, sharper picture. However, you can get good results with these steps, even if you don't have one of these attachments.

HINT

Clean Glass
Start by cleaning the scanner glass. Take color slides out of their paper or plastic mounts so they lie flat. For tips on scanning negatives, look at the next task, "Making a Positive from a Negative."

TIP

Another Route
You can also do the steps described here with the menu commands **File**, **Import**, **WIA Support** or **File**, **Import**, **WIA-<*scanner name*>**.

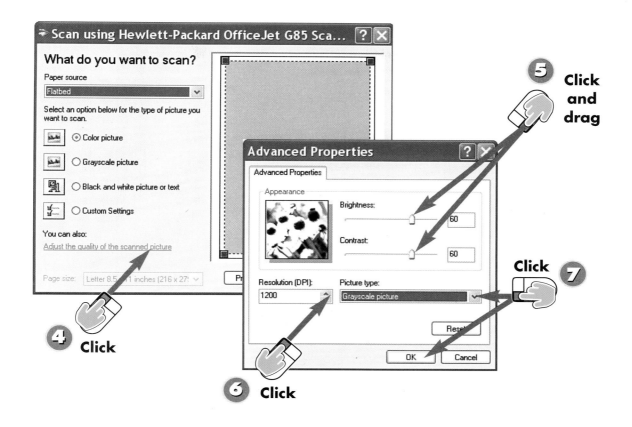

See next page

④ Click **Adjust the Quality of the Scanned Picture** (or its equivalent; the dialog window for your scanner might look different).

⑤ Increase the values of **Brightness** and **Contrast**, especially if you don't have a transparency attachment.

⑥ Increase the **Resolution** to at least **300 dpi** or more.

⑦ In the **Picture Type** drop-down menu, select **Grayscale Picture** for black-and-white originals with shading, or **Color**, and click **OK**.

TIP

Setting the DPI
In step 6, the smaller the transparency, the higher the dpi setting should be. For 35mm color slides, set the **Resolution** as high as it will go—**1200 dpi** on this scan-

HINT

ner.

It's Not All Black and White
In step 7, avoid the Black and White setting. The only time you'd use it would be for scanning line art, drawings, and

8 text that have no shading.

Click **Preview** (repeat steps 5–7 and adjust until the preview image looks right).

9 Click **Scan**. The scanned picture appears in the active image window.

End

Making Adjustments

Adjusting brightness and contrast can help compensate for not having an adapter to backlight the transparency. Get the best image you can in step 9, and then you can make further adjustments after the picture is in Photoshop Elements.

Outside Help

If you have a lot of slides, you might consider having your local photo lab convert them all to a photo CD. It'll save you the time and hassle of scanning them individually, and you'll have high-quality digital files.

Making a Positive from a Negative

Start

Click
1

Click
2

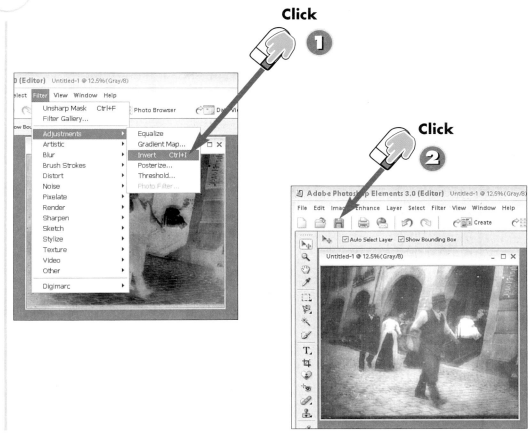

1 After you've scanned the negative, select **Filter**, **Adjustments**, **Invert** from the menu bar (or press **Ctrl+I**).

2 Click **Save** on the Shortcuts bar to save your work.

End

INTRODUCTION

It's usually easier to scan photographic prints, but Photoshop Elements can handle negatives, as well. Grayscale images work best. Scanning color negatives won't work very well unless your scanner has settings for eliminating their orange background.

HINT

Color Negatives
If you have a color print, scan that instead. If you don't have a color print and don't want to incur the expense to get one made, consult your scanner's manual to see whether it has settings for color negatives.

Importing an Acrobat Image

Start

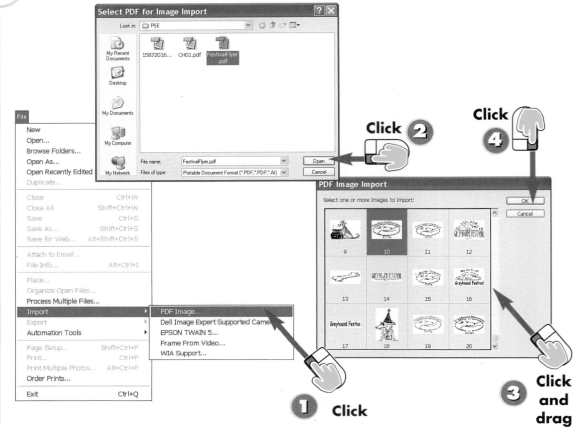

1. From the Photoshop Elements menu bar, select **File**, **Import**, **PDF Image**.

2. Select the file that contains the image you want. (If necessary, navigate the filesystem to open the folder that holds the file.) Click **Open**.

3. In the PDF Image Import window, click and drag the scrollbar to browse through the images in the file.

4. When you see the image you want, click **OK**. It will open for editing in a new 'active image window.

End

INTRODUCTION

Adobe's Acrobat Portable Document Format (**.pdf** extension) makes it possible to distribute printed brochures and manuals in electronic form. Adobe provides Acrobat Reader software free, and PDF files have become very popular on the Web. Photoshop Elements offers this built-in method for extracting pictures easily from downloaded PDF files.

Well Illustrated

HINT

You can also follow these steps to import images from Adobe Illustrator (**.ai**) documents. Other Adobe graphics applications can read and write Illustrator files, including InDesign, PageMaker, and FrameMaker.

Resizing and Printing an Image

Start

Click ①

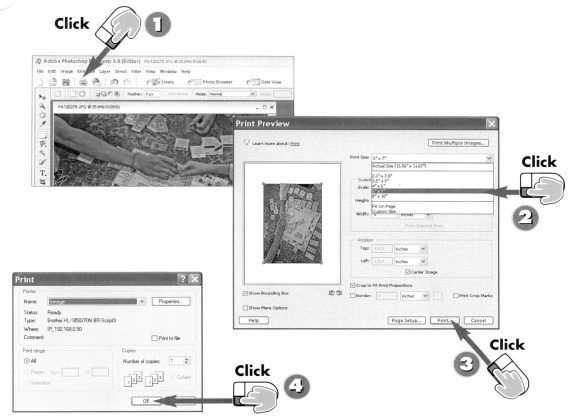

Click ②

Click ③

Click ④

① Click the **Print** button in the shortcuts bar.

② Choose a size from the **Print Size** menu.

③ Click **Print**.

④ Click **OK**.

End

INTRODUCTION

Photoshop Elements reports the current print size of the image in the lower-left corner of the work area. With these few steps, you can resize the image to fit exactly on the printed page. This method uses the default paper size currently set for the printer.

TIP

Switch Orientations
The default printer orientation is Portrait (long side vertical). To switch to Landscape (long side horizontal), after step 2, click the **Page Setup** button, select **Landscape**, click **OK**, and then go to step 3.

HINT

Glossy Prints
For the best-quality prints on a color inkjet printer, use glossy photo paper. Remove the plain paper and feed just one sheet at a time, because the glossy surface can stick to other sheets and cause jams.

Printing Contact Sheets

Start

Click ①

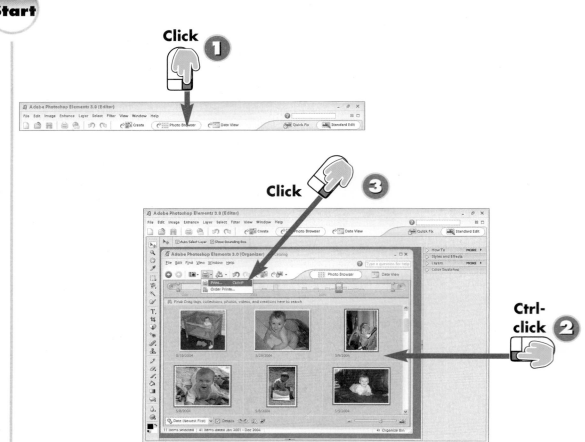

Click ③

Ctrl-click ②

① Click the **Photo Browser** button to switch to Organizer.

② Select the photos you want to include in the contact sheet.

③ Select **Print** or press **Ctrl+P**.

Professional photographers routinely make contact sheets by printing negatives laid directly on photosensitive paper. Photoshop Elements will generate contact sheets that automatically show thumbnails with labels of any group of files you select.

Get the Contact
Print and store contact sheets with each of your photo archive CDs. It's a handy way of browsing the images when they're no longer on your hard drive.

Preview First
Save paper by using the preview area in the Print Selected Photos dialog box to see how many photos appear on the last page of your contact sheets. If there's just one or two, consider reducing the number of columns.

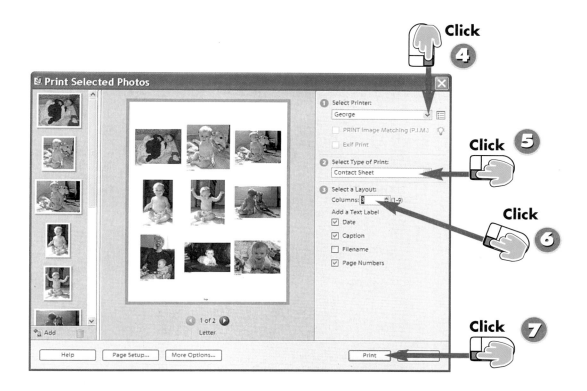

4 Select a printer.

5 Select **Contact Sheet** from the **Select Type of Print** menu.

6 Select a layout, based on the size you want the photos to be on the contact sheet.

7 Load your printer with photo paper and click **Print**.

Useful Captions
For more descriptive captions, rename camera files in Windows Explorer or in the browser before you generate the sheets.

Out of a Jam
The thumbnails of the selected files won't necessarily fit on a single contact sheet. If they don't, Photoshop Elements will print multiple sheets. Remember, to avoid printer jams, load photo paper manually, one sheet at a time.

Printing a Picture Package

Start

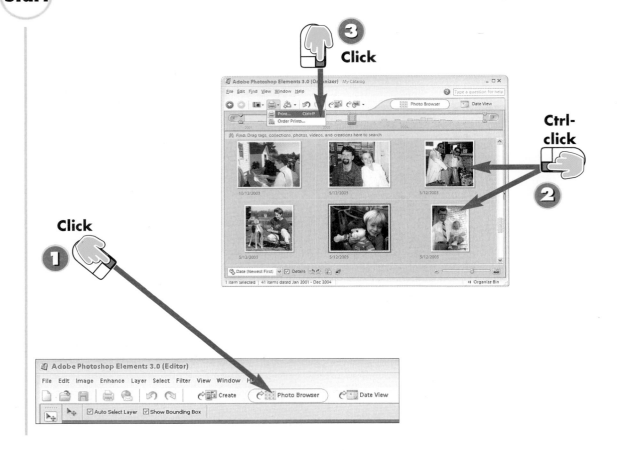

Click

Ctrl-click

Click

1. Click the **Photo Browser** button to switch to Organizer.

2. Select one or more photos to include in the picture package.

3. Click **Print** or press **Ctrl+P**.

HINT

Just Like a Pro
Have your subjects pick the shots they want from a contact sheet, then make up their picture packages. Use bright-white, glossy photo paper, and feed one sheet at a time to avoid printer jams.

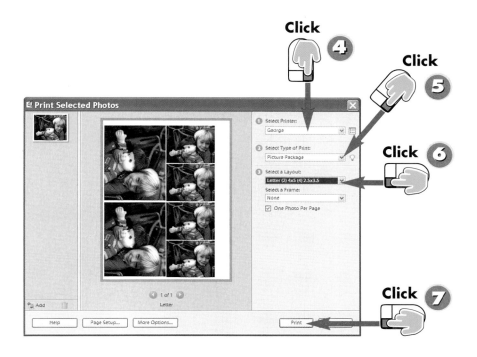

Click ④

Click ⑤

Click ⑥

Click ⑦

④ Select a printer.

⑤ Select **Picture Package** from the **Select Type of Print** menu.

⑥ Select a layout. If you're printing just one photo, check the box marked **One Photo per Page**.

⑦ Load your printer with photo paper and click **Print**.

End

Choose Your Size

TIP
If you're printing more than one photo, drag the photos in the preview area to change which photo is used for each size the layout includes.

Getting Framed

HINT
Don't forget to try the frame options available for picture package layouts. They range from actual frames (such as Country) to sophisticated edge treatments (such as Painted Edge).

Saving Your Picture Archive on CD

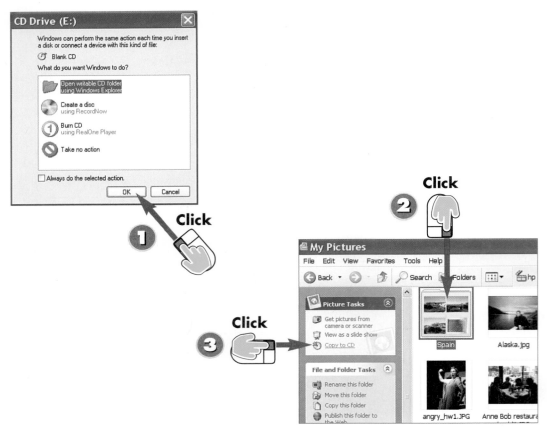

① Insert a blank CD into your CD-ROM burner and click **OK** to confirm the default choice (**Open Writable CD Folder Using Windows Explorer**).

② Locate and click the folder that contains the images you want to copy.

③ In the Picture Tasks menu, select **Copy to CD**.

Just Hold It
The capacity of a typical CD is 700MB, or enough to store 1,400 average-sized JPEG files. If you have a DVD burner, you can put 4GB (about 8,000 shots) on a single DVD-R data disc (but don't put all your precious photos on one disc).

Write It Again
You can add files to CD-R discs until they are full, if your burner supports multi-session capability. You can both add and overwrite files on CD-RW discs (a few times, not indefinitely).

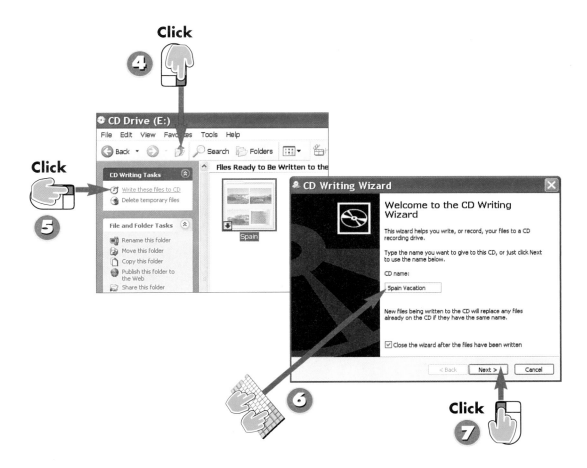

Click

4 In Windows Explorer, navigate the filesystem to reopen the CD directory.

5 In the CD Writing Tasks menu, select **Write These Files to CD**.

6 Click the text box and type a label for the CD, such as **Spain Vacation**.

7 Click **Next**. The disc will eject when copying is complete.

End

Get It Together
If your photos aren't all in a single folder, copy them all to a single temporary folder first. Alternatively, select a collection of them in Explorer by pressing **Ctrl-click**. Then select **Edit**, **Copy**; navigate to the CD drive; and select **Edit**, **Paste**.

Out of the Window
Instead of using the built-in copying functions of Windows XP, you could use a CD-burning application such as Roxio Easy CD Creator or Veritas RecordNow.

Basic Photo Fixing

Think of this part of the book as a comfy family restaurant where you could go for your daily bread and never be bored with the same meal twice. It's just not slick, or complicated, or arty. (Oh, we'll go there, too, eventually.) You'd be well served to return here again and again—but these steps are so quick and easy that to do them once is to know them cold.

Up to this point, you've opened files and printed them out, but you haven't changed how they look very much. If you need to fix a photo, come here first. Your quest will probably end here, and you'll be more than satisfied. The shot that looked too dark will perk right up, crooked will become straight, and that unflattering pallor on her face will become a rosy glow.

A particularly handy feature of Photoshop Elements is the Quick Fix workspace, which gives you single-click access to a variety of commonly needed repairs—with automatic corrections. The first two tasks in this part demonstrate its use.

So, if you have time to do only a few of the tasks in this book, choose some of these. You'll be hooked, and you'll recover a lot of shots you thought were duds.

Applying Quick and Easy Fixes

Before

After

Making a Quick Fix

Start

Click

Click

4

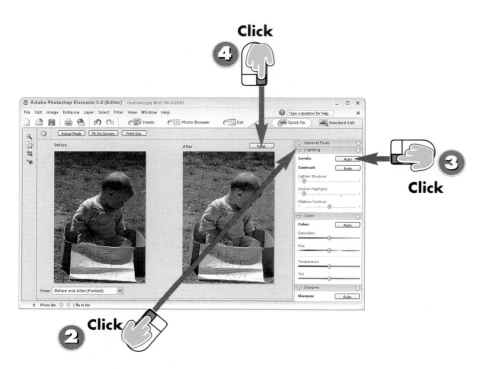

Click

3

Click

Click

2

1 With the picture you want to fix in the active image area, click the **Quick Fix** button on the shortcuts bar.

2 Click the disclosure triangle for the section you want to use (such as **Lighting**).

3 Click an **Auto** button (such as **Levels**) to adjust the image; Levels adjusts the picture's balance of dark and light areas.

4 If you don't like the changes Elements makes, click **Reset** to restore the image to original state.

End

You can use Photoshop Elements's Quick Fix mode as one-stop-shopping for all the commands in the Enhance menu. Get there by clicking the **Quick Fix** button on the shortcuts bar, or by clicking **Quickly Fix Photos** in the Welcome screen.

Auto and Semi-Auto Fixes
Any of the Auto adjustments require just a single click of the button. If you want more control over the changes, you can use the sliders to determine the amount of modification made to lighting and color and the amount of sharpening.

Don't Like *After*?
Your Quick Fix changes are cumulative, so you can do one, such as Auto Lighting, and then do another, such as a custom amount of sharpening applied with the slider—until the After image is just right.

Making a Quick Fix with a Slider Adjustment

Start

Click ➊

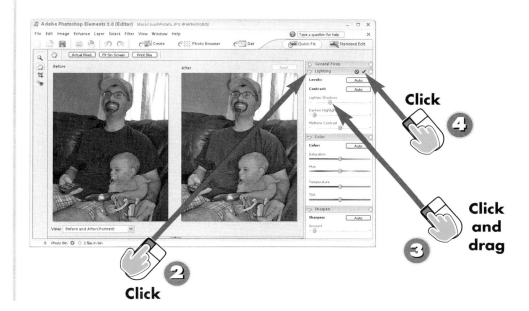

Click ➋

Click ➍

Click and drag ➌

➊ With the picture you want to fix in the active image area, click the **Quick Fix** button on the shortcuts bar.

➋ Click the disclosure triangle to open the Quick Fix section you want to use.

➌ Drag a slider to adjust the image.

➍ Click the **Commit** button (✔) when you like the way the After image looks.

End

Elements's Auto functions are pretty good—but they're not perfect because the program doesn't really know what each image is supposed to look like. Only you know that, which is why you often get better results by adjusting a picture's color, lighting, and sharpness yourself.

Cancel That
Next to the Commit button is a Cancel button; click it to remove the effects of the most recent change you made to the picture without reverting completely.

The Color of Light
Use the Color section's Temperature and Tint sliders as a quick fix for bad lighting. Photos taken under incandescent light lose their yellow cast if you drag the Temperature slider toward the Cool end.

Fixing Everything

Start

Click ①

Click ③

Click ②

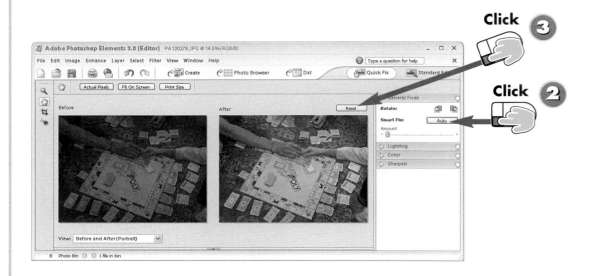

① With the picture you want to fix in the active image area, click the **Quick Fix** button on the shortcuts bar.

② Click the **Auto Smart Fix** button to adjust the image's color, lighting, and sharpness all at once.

③ If you don't like the changes Elements makes, click **Reset** to restore the image to its original state.

End

The Smart Fix feature adjusts every aspect of the image, based on Photoshop Elements's idea of what the ideal picture should look like. It's a great way to get an idea of how much improvement you'll be able to make in a photo, even if you opt to use the Reset button and make each adjustment manually for greater control.

More Fun with Quick Fix
In addition to the quick fixes shown here, you can also crop pictures and remove red-eye in Quick Fix mode by using the Crop and Red Eye Removal tools at the left side of the work area.

Getting a Good View
Use the Zoom and Hand tools at the left of the work area to zoom in and out and move the picture around. That way, you can get a good idea of how your changes are affecting different areas of the image.

Undoing Your Mistakes

Click

Click

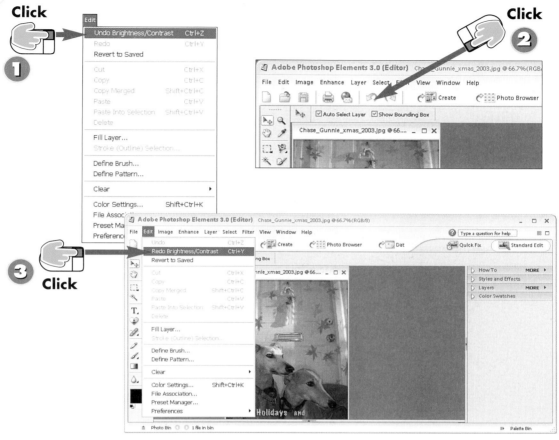

Click

1 Immediately after making any change to the picture in the active image area, choose **Edit**, **Undo**, or press **Alt+Ctrl+Z**.

2 To undo the next-most-recent change, click the **Step Backward** shortcut (or choose **Edit**, **Step Backward**, or press **Ctrl+Z**).

3 To reapply the last change you undid, choose **Edit**, **Redo**, or press **Alt+Ctrl+Z** before you do anything else.

End

INTRODUCTION

Don't think of any photo-fixing decisions you make as mistakes, for two good reasons: You can always undo them, and experimenting is the only way to learn what works and what doesn't. So, click away—you have nothing to lose but playtime!

TIP

Other Ways to Undo
As alternatives, you can use the Step Backward and Step Forward shortcuts, or open the **Undo History** palette. Right-click the step you want to undo, and select **Delete** (subsequent steps are deleted, too).

HINT

Canceling All Changes
To undo all your changes during a session—*before* you save—choose **File**, **Revert**. The last saved version of the file appears in the active image area.

Cropping a Picture

Start

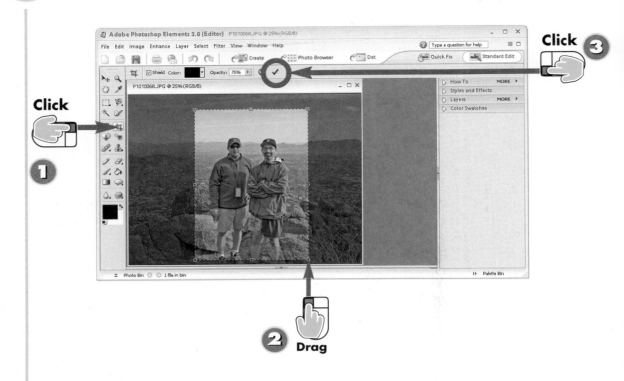

Click ③

Click

①

② Drag

① Select the **Crop** tool from the toolbox, or press **C**.

② Within the active image area, drag the corner of a selection box to indicate the new framing.

③ Click the **Commit** button in the options bar, or press **Enter**.

End

One hallmark of a skilled photographer is pleasing *composition*, or arrangement of the things you're shooting within the picture frame. You can't always take the time to get the composition just right. Cropping used to be one of the most common fixes made in the darkroom—now you can do it with the lights on.

Adjusting Width and Height
After step 1, type a Width and Height in the options bar to match the proportions (type **5** for Width and **7** for Height for a 5×7 print). Or, pressing **Shift** while dragging forces a perfectly square selection.

Canceling the Crop
In step 3, to cancel the cropping operation, click the **Cancel** button (just left of the Commit button) in the options bar or press **Esc**.

Straightening a Crooked Picture

Start

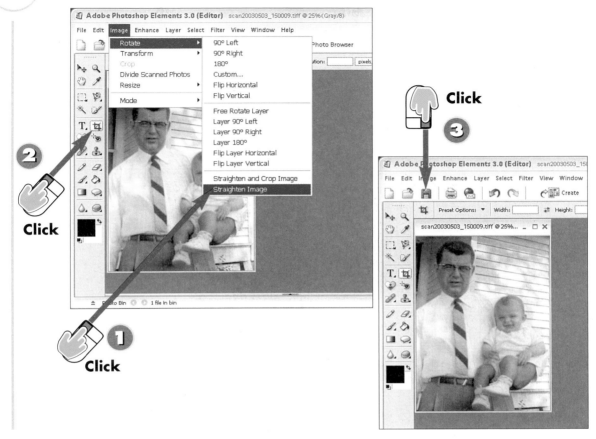

Click ②

Click ①

Click ③

1. With the picture in the active image area, choose **Image**, **Rotate**, **Straighten Image**. The program aligns the image.

2. Crop the photo as desired.

3. Click the **Save** shortcut to save your changes.

End

INTRODUCTION

This type of automatic straightening works best when the subject is just slightly out of alignment—a tower that appears to be leaning, for example. The program finds a strong vertical or horizontal line in the image and aligns it on the nearest 90° angle.

TIP

Severely Off-Angle?
If the subject is severely off angle, use one of the **Image**, **Rotate** or **Image**, **Transform** commands instead.

HINT

Straighten *and* Crop
As an alternative, the program can both straighten *and* crop automatically (choose **Image**, **Rotate**, **Straighten and Crop Image**). But you'll be happier with the results if you crop it yourself.

Rotating an Image on Opening

Start

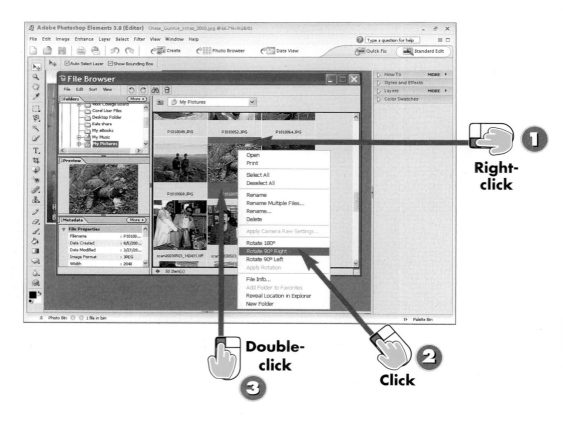

Right-click ①

Double-click ③

Click ②

① In the File Browser, right-click the thumbnail of the picture you want to rotate.

② Select a rotation angle, such as **Rotate 90° Right**. (If you see a message screen, click **OK**.)

③ Double-click the thumbnail to open the file for editing.

End

Like film cameras, digital cameras take all pictures in landscape orientation—with the long side of the frame horizontal. To take a portrait, you must physically rotate the camera. The most common reason to rotate an image in Photoshop Elements is so that you can view it correctly for editing and printing.

Quick and Easy Rotation

This method of rotating a picture has the same effect as selecting one of the **Image**, **Rotate** commands from the menu bar. But you'll find it's more convenient for quickly rotating all your portrait shots.

If you Ctrl-click multiple thumbnails before you do step 1, you can apply the same rotation to multiple shots with a single command. But you must then open the files individually.

Rotating an Image for Artistic Effect

Start

Click ①

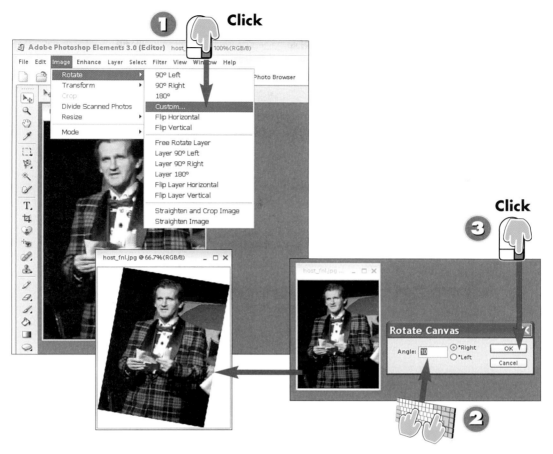

Click ③

②

① With the picture in the active image area, choose **Image**, **Rotate**, **Custom**.

② In the Rotate Canvas box, type a rotation angle in degrees (clockwise from 12 o'clock; or, click **Left** for counterclockwise rotation).

③ Click **OK**.

End

INTRODUCTION

Graphic artists call this type of rotation a *Dutch angle*. Perhaps the most familiar example is the nightclub poster with rotated glamour portraits of the performers. It's a great technique for adding flair to greeting cards and family Web pages.

HINT

Auto-Adjust Canvas Size
Photoshop Elements automatically increases the canvas size to create a frame large enough to hold the rotated picture without reducing the image size. The area outside the picture is the current background color.

TIP

Continuous Rotation
As an alternative, you can choose **Image**, **Rotate**, **Free Rotate Layer** and drag a corner to rotate the image continuously. However, this way does *not* increase the canvas size, and some cropping of the picture corners occurs.

Resizing and Resampling an Image

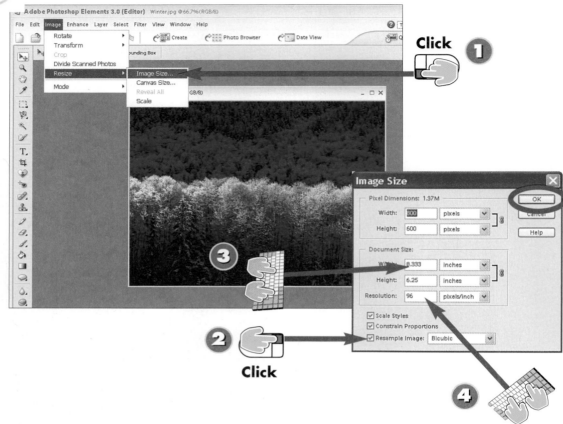

Click ①

Click ②

③

④

① With a picture in the active image area, choose **Image**, **Resize**, **Image Size**.

② Click **Resample Image**.

③ Type a new width in the box, in decimal units (such as inches).

④ Select the **Resolution** box and type a new numeric value, such as **96** pixels/inch. Click **OK**.

End

Digital photos are composed of a finite number of pixels. Resizing and resampling often go hand in hand: If you increase the size of an image, the result can look coarse unless you resample it to increase the resolution. If you reduce the image size, it decreases the resolution, resulting in a smaller file size.

Enter Width or Height
In step 3, enter Width or Height, but not both. If you enter one, the program calculates the other so that the image isn't distorted. The Resolution value should be 72 for email or the Web, 150–300 for making prints with a color inkjet.

Bicubic Is Best
For all but the slowest computers or very large images, leave the Resample Image option set to Bicubic, which gives the highest-quality result. Bilinear, which takes less processing time, is the next-best choice.

Removing Objects from an Image

Start

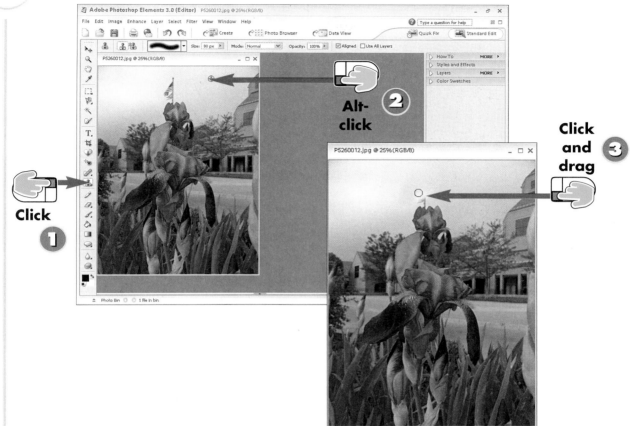

Click 1

Alt-click 2

Click and drag 3

1 Select the **Clone Stamp** tool from the toolbox, or press **S**.

2 Press **Alt** as you click a clear area that matches the background.

3 Click and drag over the object you want to remove from the image.

End

To take a great photo, you have to catch both the subject and the setting at just the right time. If another object intrudes into the scene at the crucial second, Photoshop Elements makes it easy to remove that little "extra" at a later date.

HINT

Take Your Time
You might need to apply the Clone Stamp multiple times, using short strokes, to blend the new pixels in with the existing background.

HINT

Object Removal Magic
The Clone Stamp tool is a good choice for removing objects on irregular backgrounds, and for larger objects. For small objects, Elements includes special "healing" tools. Turn to "Removing Facial Blemishes," **p.133**, to learn more.

Transforming Image Perspective

Start

Click **1**

Click **2**

Click **3**

1 With a picture in the active image area, choose **Image**, **Transform**, **Perspective**.

2 Click **OK** on the warning dialog box.

3 The layer is automatically named Layer 0. Click **OK**.

INTRODUCTION

The Image, Transform submenu actually has three other commands besides Perspective: Free Transform, Skew, and Distort. But you apply them all the same way—by dragging picture corners. Try each of them using these steps to see how their effects differ.

TIP

Severe Distortion?
Severe distortion on subjects such as tall buildings results not only from perspective but also from an effect of optical lenses called barrel distortion—which adds curvature.

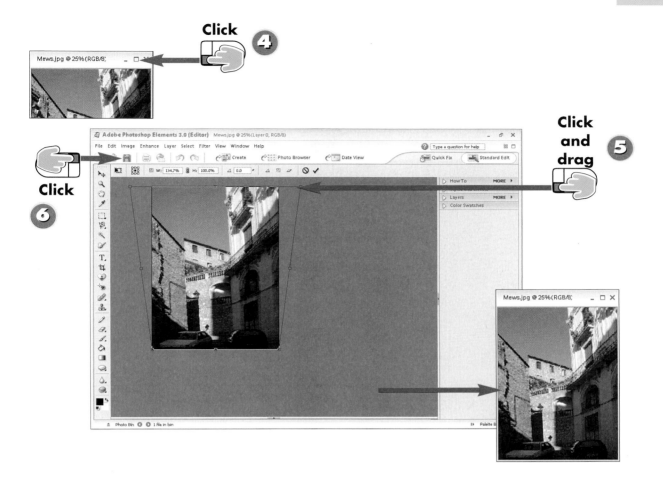

4 Click the **Maximize** button to enlarge the active image area.

5 Click and drag a corner to adjust the perspective.

6 **Save** the transformed image.

Watch for Keystoning
Keystoning, another type of distortion, results from aiming the camera either up or down at a severe angle. To compensate for keystoning, drag the corner in step 5 that's nearest the pinched end of the subject outward.

Don't Squish Your Folks
Be careful that in removing distortion from one part of a picture, such as the slope of a building, you don't add distortion in another part—squishing cars or, worse, the faces of your loved ones.

Adding a White Border to Your Prints

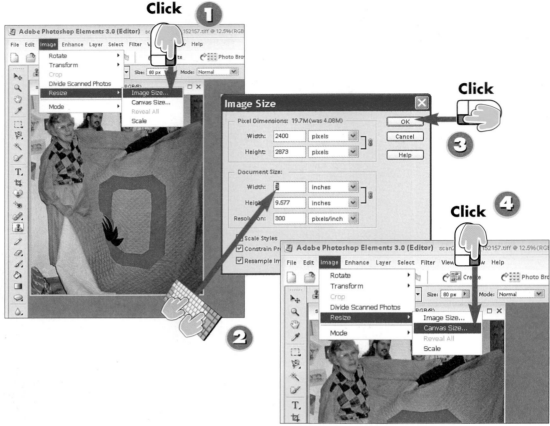

Click ①

Click ③

Click ④

②

① With a picture in the active image area, choose **Image**, **Resize**, **Image Size**.

② Type the new image width as a decimal, such as **8** inches.

③ Click **OK**.

④ Choose **Image**, **Resize**, **Canvas Size**.

INTRODUCTION

A good way to add a white border to your prints involves resizing the image to be smaller than the canvas (paper) size by the amount of the margin you want, and centering the image on the canvas.

When to Resample
In step 2, check **Resample Image** and increase the resolution if the number in the Resolution field is less than 150. To avoid distorting the image, let the program calculate the height.

Yet Another Way
To add a white border without resizing the canvas, choose **File**, **Print Preview**. Check the **Show More Options** check box; then click the **Border** button. You can specify the width of the border in inches, millimeters, or points.

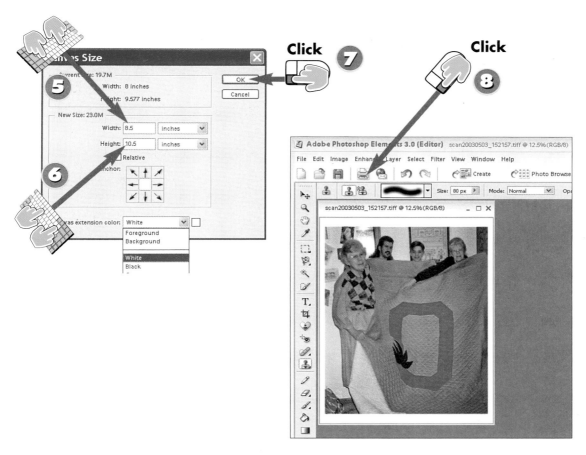

5. In the **Width** box, type the width of the print paper—larger than the image width—such as **8.5** inches.

6. In the **Height** box, type the height of the paper, such as **10.5** inches.

7. Click **OK**.

8. Load the printer with photo paper and click **Print**.

Note the Printable Area
The border becomes part of the image file, so you shouldn't have to adjust print margins as long as the *printable area* of your paper matches the canvas size. Use these steps to add borders to the pictures you print with the File, Print Layouts, Picture Package command, which uses standard print sizes.

What's the Anchor Point?
The *anchor point* indicates the position of the image relative to the canvas edges. The default is centered. Also remember that most printers can't make borderless prints, so you'll have to allow for the printer's built-in margins.

Removing "Red Eye" in Flash Photos

Start

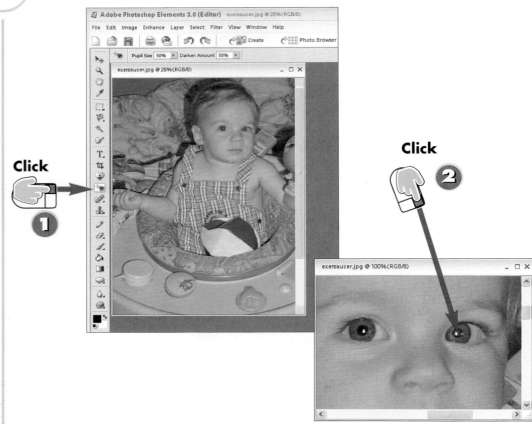

Click

1

Click

2

End

1 With the photo that needs fixing in the active image area, select the **Red Eye Removal** tool, or press **Y**.

2 Click the red area in the photo to select the color you want to remove.

The telltale red-eye effect happens when the flash is mounted on or built into the camera and the subject is looking directly into the lens. The retina of the eye bounces the light right back. Take these steps to dispel those smoldering looks.

Zooming Will Help
This task is much easier if you *zoom* your view of the eye so that you can see the detail before you apply the brush. If the effect is tiny, you may be able to wash it out with a single click—no scrubbing.

Multicolored Reflections?
Remember that this command only replaces a single color. Red-eye reflections may actually be multicolored. Repeat these steps for each individual color you need to remove.

Correcting a Color Cast

Start

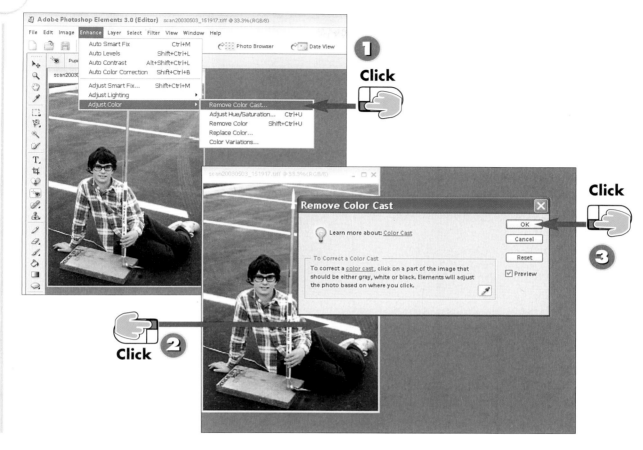

Click

Click

Click

With a picture in the active image area, choose **Enhance**, **Adjust Color**, **Remove Color Cast**.

Click an area of the image that should be white.

Click **OK**.

End

Pick Pure White
In step 2, pick an area such as teeth, white of the eye, or a white tablecloth or shirt collar. Any blown-out (overexposed) area usually gives the best result. If there's no white anywhere in the picture, click a neutral area (gray or black).

Selecting Color Variations

Start

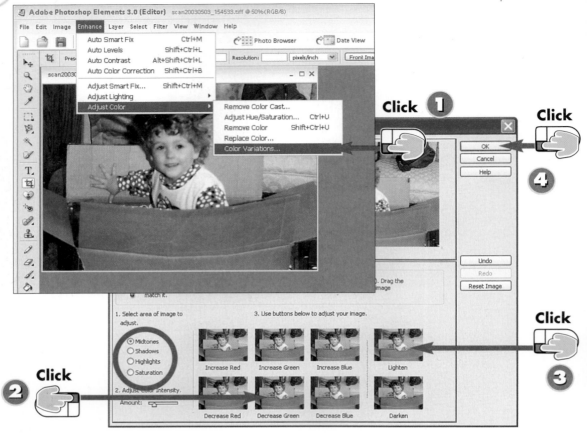

Click ①

Click

Click

Click

Click ②

② ③ ④

Increase Red Increase Green Increase Blue Lighten

Decrease Red Decrease Green Decrease Blue Darken

① With a picture in the active image area, select **Enhance**, **Adjust Color**, **Color Variations**.

② Click a thumbnail, such as **Decrease Green**, to change color or brightness in the shot.

③ Repeat the same selection to increase its effect, or make any other selection, such as **Lighten**, for a combined effect.

④ When the After image looks right, click **OK**.

End

Perhaps it's not that the colors in the picture are wrong, you'd just like to see them different. For example, an interior decorator might want to view a room in a different light or with the decor a different shade. Experiment with color variations, which can be more dramatic than just correcting the overall cast.

TIP

Adjust Midtones First
Of the selections Midtones, Shadows, Highlights, and Saturation, Midtones (values ranging between shadows and highlights) usually give you the most noticeable results. To change the magnitude of an effect, drag the **Adjust Color Intensity** slider before you apply it.

Replacing a Specific Color

Start

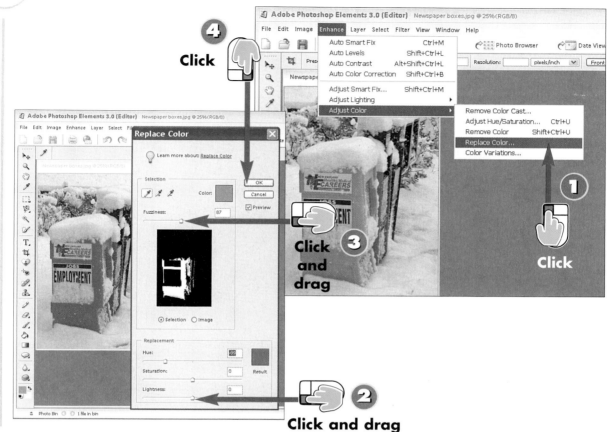

Click

Click and drag

Click and drag

Click

Click

1 With a picture in the active image area, choose **Enhance**, **Adjust Color**, **Replace Color**.

2 Click within an area in the picture; then click and drag the **Replacement** sliders until you see the color you want in the Sample box.

3 Click and drag the **Fuzziness** slider to recolor all similar shades in the selection.

4 Click **OK**.

End

INTRODUCTION

Don't like the color of that dress? Does the sofa clash with the drapes? Want to make the sky pink or the river run green? You can make it so at no extra charge—with your choices limited only by your fashion sense.

TIP

Add or Subtract
Click the **Add to Sample** or **Subtract from Sample** eyedroppers (marked with + and −) and click the area in the picture to add or remove it. Then, dragging the Transform sliders applies the color change to the entire selection.

HINT

What Changes?
These steps change all instances of the same color anywhere in the image, not just on the area you select in step 2.

Adjusting Brightness and Contrast

Start

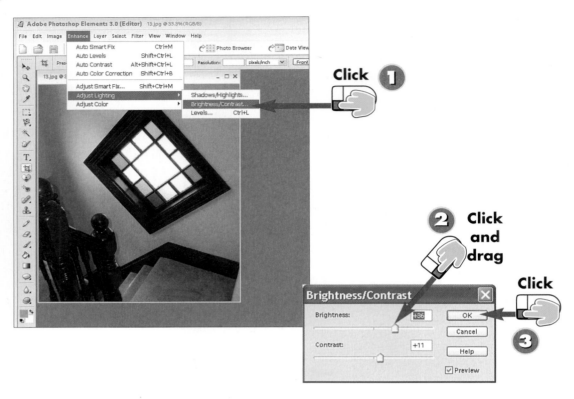

Click ①

Click and drag ②

Click ③

① With a picture in the active image area, choose **Enhance**, **Adjust Lighting**, **Brightness/Contrast**.

② Click and drag one or both sliders, **Brightness** and/or **Contrast**, until the picture looks right.

③ Click **OK**.

End

Sometimes a Quick Fix like Auto Contrast just doesn't do the trick—especially if the image has bright highlights, deep shadows, or both. These steps give you more control so that you can make continuous adjustments while previewing the result.

Overall Change

Changing brightness and contrast affects the entire image unless you select a particular area first. Selection tools are Rectangular Marquee (for rectangular areas), Lasso (for irregular areas), and Magic Wand (for intricate shapes).

Subject in the Dark?

If your subject is too dark overall (underexposed), try the Fill Flash fix first. It boosts brightness only in the darker areas, leaving the lighter areas—usually, the background—alone.

Changing a Color Photo to Black and White

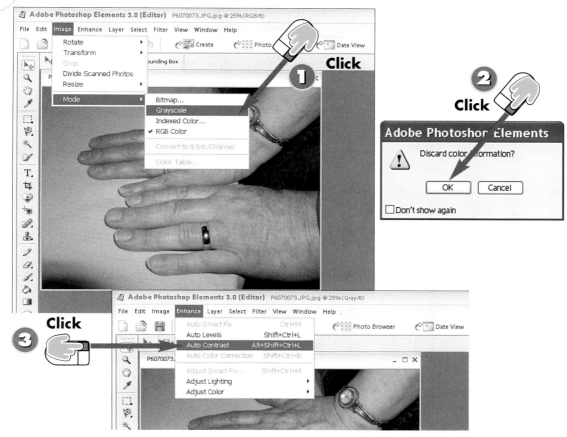

Click

Click

Click

1 With a color picture in the active image area, choose **Image**, **Mode**, **Grayscale**.

2 Click **OK**.

3 Choose **Enhance**, **Auto Contrast**.

End

You'll occasionally need black-and-white pictures for newsletters that will be printed one-color—or perhaps when you're in a vintage-movie kind of mood. You can easily convert your color shots to B&W, but remember to finish by adjusting the contrast to make them suitably snappy.

Sepia (a brownish monochrome) is actually a color effect. After converting to B&W and adjusting contrast, repeat the **Image**, **Mode** command and select **RGB Color**; then apply one or more **Color Variations**.

Sharpening Focus

Start

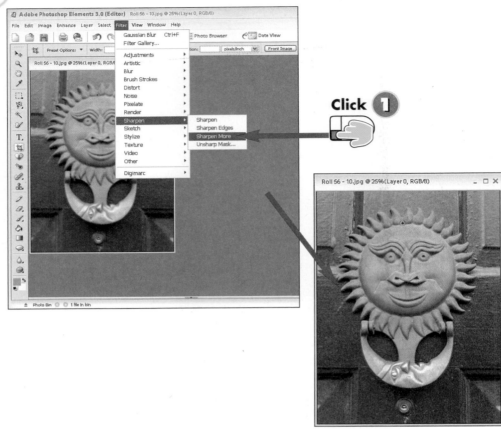

Click 1

1 With a picture in the active image area, choose **Filter**, **Sharpen**, **Sharpen More**.

End

Digital cameras have an *auto-focus* feature, which attempts to make the edges of the subject in the center of the frame as sharp as possible. It doesn't always work. For more consistent results, learn how to focus manually. But you can always try this simple step to sharpen shots that are slightly blurred.

Focus Manually
The Sharpen command can improve the look of a blurred shot somewhat, but it's no substitute for proper manual focusing. That's particularly true when you're doing *closeups*—with the subject less than four feet away.

Don't Overdo It
This task uses Sharpen More because you might not see much of a difference from the original when you use the Sharpen submenu command. And Sharpen Edges can overdo it.

Making Edges Softer

Start

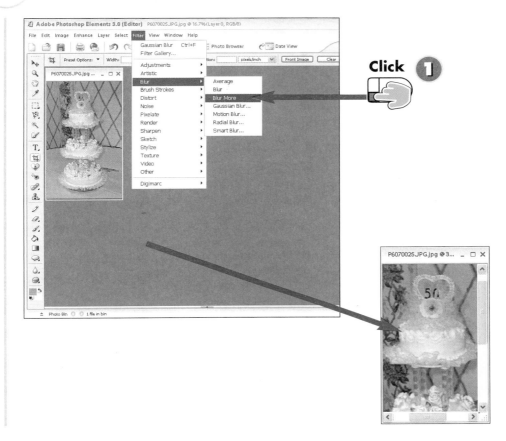

Click 1

1 With a picture in the active image area, choose **Filter**, **Blur**, **Blur More**.

End

INTRODUCTION

There are at least two good reasons to soften focus: It can make a portrait look more flattering, blending out lines, pores, and small blemishes; and it can save a shot that's only slightly out of focus—making the softness look more deliberate.

TIP

An Artful Blur
This task uses Blur More because the result of the Blur command in the submenu can be hard to see. The other Blur commands in the submenu are for when you're feeling arty.

Selecting and Coloring Shapes in the Shot

Start

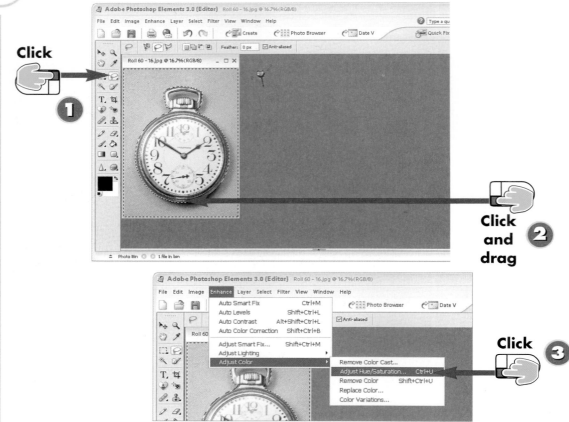

Click ①

Click and drag ②

Click ③

① With a picture in the active image area, select the **Lasso** tool.

② Click and drag in the image to trace the outline of the area you want to change.

③ Choose **Enhance**, **Adjust Color**, **Adjust Hue/Saturation**.

INTRODUCTION

By using one of the selection tools first, you can apply any of the color, brightness, and level commands to specific areas within an image. In this example, a portion of the background didn't contrast well with the subject, so it was recolored.

HINT

Practice Your Selections
Using the selection tools to capture just the pixels you want to change and no others is a mark of skill with Photoshop Elements. Remember, you can use the selection tools in any sequence for a combined result, to add or subtract from the current selection.

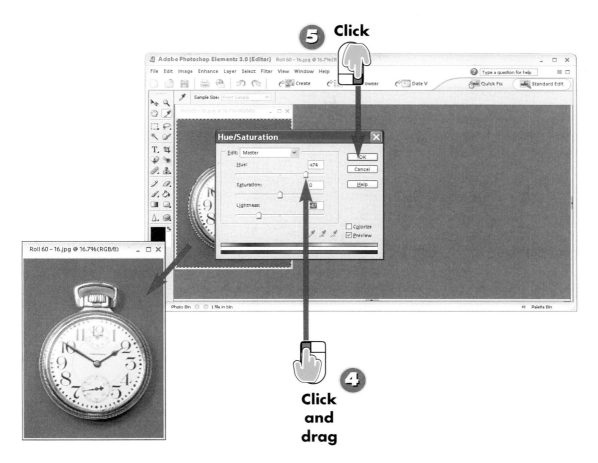

Click

Click and drag

4 Click and drag one or more sliders, such as **Hue**, to adjust the color of the selected area.

5 Click **OK**.

End

Colorizing Gets Garish
Checking the Colorize box in the Hue/Saturation window gives you a wider range of colors, many of them garish. By decreasing Saturation, you can also experiment with the Colorize option to create *duo-tone* (two-color) pictures.

Do Sweat the Small Stuff
Notice how the background that's visible within the watch's bow (the ring) is still off-white? That's because it wasn't included in the selection made in step 2. Watch out for these small gotchas.

Using the Eyedroppers
In step 4, the eyedroppers become available when you select something other than Master in the Edit drop-down box. Do this to adjust primary colors separately in the image, or to recolor specific areas you sample with the eyedropper.

Adding Titles and Text

Being able to print text on your photos can turn your digital snaps into greeting cards, invitations, postcards, or posters.

An interesting photo with a caption can be a news item for a community newsletter or family Web site.

And even if you don't aspire to craft your own greetings or write your own news, including captions in your picture files is a much better way of identifying and describing your photos than writing on the back of the prints with a ballpoint pen.

As you gain skill working with text, you'll want the flexibility of keeping different pieces of text on separate *layers*, which work like clear sheets of acetate you can draw on. Layers permit you to add text and artwork without making any permanent changes to the underlying image. So be sure to take a look at the tasks in Part 9, "Using Layers to Combine Photos and Artwork."

And don't worry. None of this is complicated. Photoshop Element's built-in features help you create professional-looking output, whether it be for a Web site or picture postcard, without having to sweat the technical details.

Say It with Pictures and Words

Don's new Kawasaki motorcycle is much redder than his previous Yamaha model.

Adding a caption can give a photo "news value."

SportsToday
December 2005

52

67

Coming Soon:
Spring Training

Why not think of your life as a game—and you're the star!

Adding and Printing Photo Captions

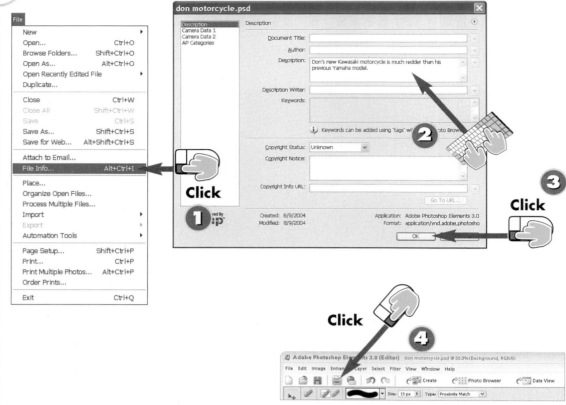

1 With the picture in the active image area, choose **File**, **File Info**.

2 Type a descriptive caption in the **Description** text box.

3 Click **OK**.

4 Click the **Print** button (or choose **File**, **Print**).

This method of adding a caption to a photo stores the text information with the image file. When you check the Caption check box in the Print Preview dialog box, your photo prints with the caption outside the image area, centered beneath it.

Dear Diary...
In step 2, the Description text box can hold about 25 double-spaced pages. That's enough to paste a whole text document from the Clipboard. You could use it to hold your journal entries from a trip, for example.

Title and Author Boxes
You can also type entries into the Document Title and Author boxes seen on the File Info dialog. However, only the Description box is printed by this procedure.

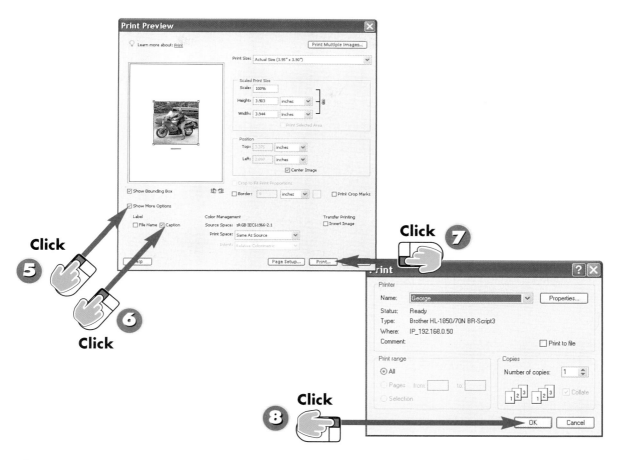

Click **5**

Click **6**

Click **7**

Click **8**

5 Check the **Show More Options** check box.

6 Check the **Caption** check box.

7 Click **Print**.

8 Click **OK** in the Print dialog box.

End

Fitting on the Page
HINT
If you haven't sized the image to fit the canvas and the canvas to the paper size, choose **Fit on Page** from the Print Size pop-up menu in the Print Preview dialog box, and Photoshop Elements fits to the paper size selected for the printer.

Overlaying Text on an Image

Start

2

Click

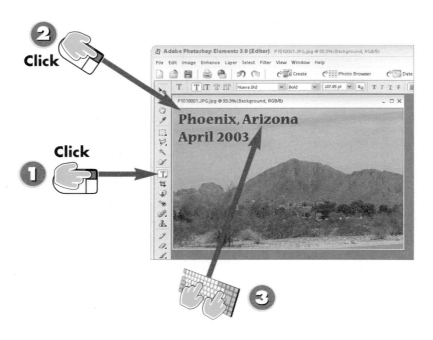

Click

1

3

1 With a picture in the active image area, select the **Horizontal Type** tool.

2 Click the position in the image where the text will begin.

3 Type a line of text. To start a second line, press **Enter** and keep typing.

End

Here's the direct approach—just type over an image anywhere you want. You can press Enter between typing multiple lines in the same block of text, or you can click Commit and then repeat these steps to create a separate block that you can move and work with independently.

Alignment Options
The starting point for the text line in step 2 depends on the current Alignment setting in the Options bar (Left Align, Centered, or Right Align).

New Text Layer
These steps create a new text layer automatically. Think of a layer as a clear sheet you can write or draw on without changing the image underneath.

Selecting and Editing Text

Start

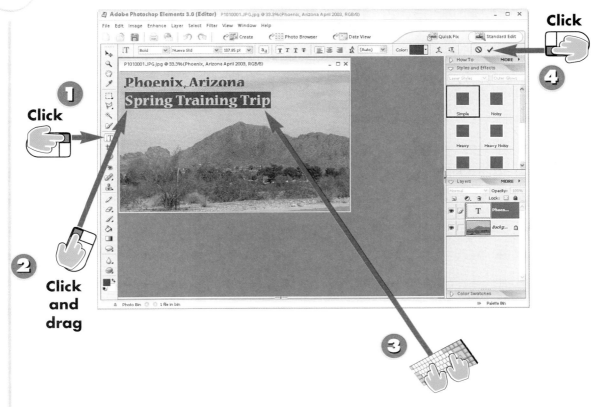

Click

1

Click

2

Click and drag

3

Click

4

1 Select the **Horizontal Type** tool.

2 Click and drag over the characters you want to replace.

3 Type the replacement characters.

4 Click the **Commit** button in the options bar.

End

A handy way to remember how to edit text is "swipe and type" because you must first highlight the letters you want to replace.

TIP

Inserting Characters
To insert one or more characters rather than replace some, just click at the insertion point in step 2 and then type.

HINT

Keep Text Editable
You can't edit text after the text layers have been merged with the image (as in a JPEG file, for example). To keep text editable, save your work as a native Photoshop file.

Changing Fonts and Text Properties

Start

2 Click and drag

Click

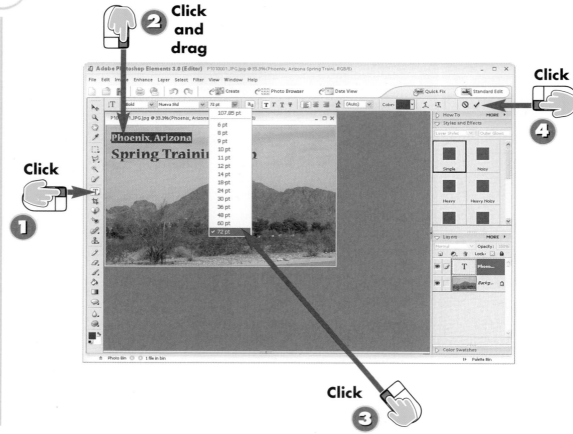

Click

1

Click

3

4

1 Select the **Horizontal Type** tool.

2 Click and drag over the characters you want to change.

3 Select new text properties from the drop-down boxes in the options bar, such as **Font Size**.

4 Click the **Commit** button in the options bar.

End

Words or even individual characters can have different properties, such as color or font, than adjacent characters in the same block.

Lines and Blocks of Text
Create the text in a single text block rather than individual ones when you want Photoshop Elements to take care of alignment and spacing between lines.

Text Properties
Settings for all text properties become available in the options bar when a text object is selected in the active image area.

Moving or Deleting Text

Start

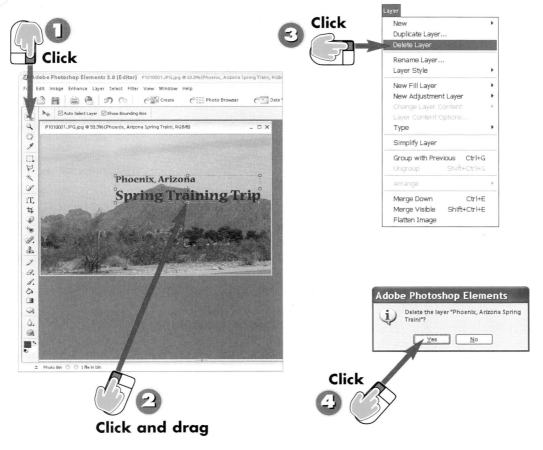

Click ①

Click and drag ②

Click ③

Click ④

① Select the **Move** tool, or press **V**.

② Click and drag the text object to a new position.

③ Or, to delete the entire text layer, choose **Layer**, **Delete Layer**.

④ Click **Yes** to confirm the deletion.

End

INTRODUCTION

You move a block of text the same way you'd move any other graphic object you create. For example, you should move a line of text out of a cluttered area of the background, to make it more readable.

TIP

Avoid Distortion
To avoid distorting the text, select the center of the object before you drag it around. Press **Shift** while you drag to force horizontal or vertical alignment, or press **Alt** to make it diagonal.

Resizing Text

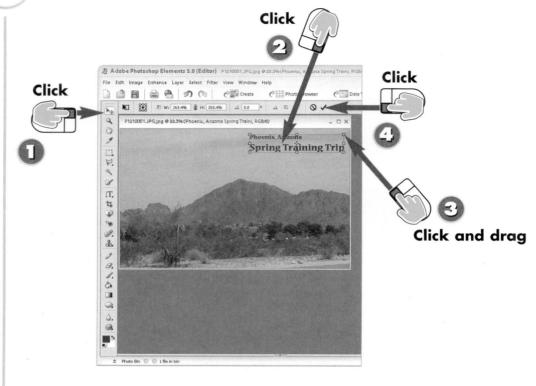

Click ②

Click ④

Click ①

Click and drag ③

Start

1 Select the **Move** tool, or press **V**.

2 Click the text object you want to resize.

3 Click and drag any handle on the selection box until the box is at the desired size.

4 Click the **Commit** button in the options bar.

End

This procedure works just like a move, but you drag a handle (corner) rather than the center of the object. It works best for condensing or extending, shrinking or enlarging text by small amounts.

TIP

Best Resizing Results
To enlarge and distort text so that its edges stay smooth, change the **Font Size** first in the options bar and then adjust slightly by dragging object handles. Or, distort with the **Image**, **Transform**, **Free Transform** command instead.

HINT

Auto Select Layer
For step 2 to work, the Auto Select Layer box must be checked in the options bar (the usual setting). If it's not checked, you must switch to the corresponding text layer using the Layers palette.

Creating Vertical Text

Start

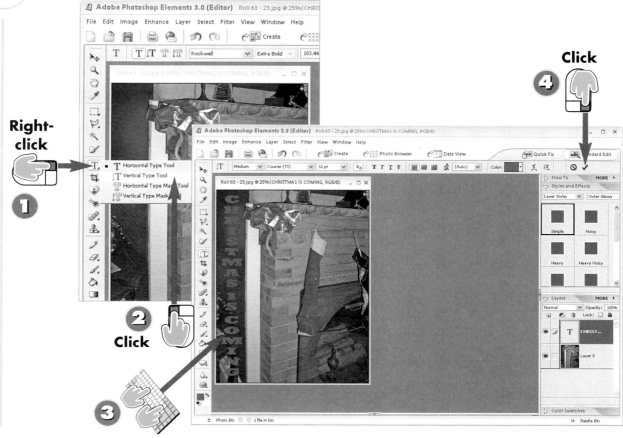

Right-click ①

Click ②

③

Click ④

1 Right-click the **Type** tool.

2 Select **Vertical Type Tool** from the submenu.

3 Click the starting point in the image and type some text.

4 Click the **Commit** button in the options bar.

End

Vertical text can be difficult to read, but there are times when it's the best fit in a tight space. Text created this way reads from the top downward.

Adding More Text Lines
Press **Enter** after step 3 to add more vertical lines of text to the same block. But for some odd reason, the lines read from right to left. (Enter the second line first if you want them to read from left to right.)

Vertical Alignment Options
Selections for vertical alignment of text in the options bar are Top Align, Center, and Bottom Align. But in all cases, text reads from the top downward.

Rotating Text

Start

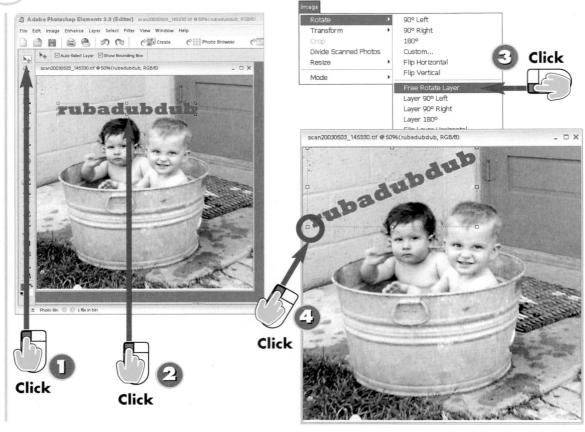

3 Click

4 Click

Click **1**

Click **2**

1 Select the **Move** tool, or press **V**.

2 Click the text object you want to rotate.

3 Choose **Image**, **Rotate**, **Free Rotate Layer**.

4 Click and drag a handle on the selection box.

End

You might want to rotate text to achieve a smarter design or to fit it to an object in the image. Just remember that it might become difficult to read if the angle is too severe.

TIP

Flipping Text
Flipping (creating a mirror-image of) text can be done by choosing **Image**, **Rotate**, **Flip Layer Horizontal** or **Flip Layer Vertical**. (Submenu commands that don't include "Layer" affect the entire image.)

HINT

Auto Select Layer
For step 2 to work, the Auto Select Layer box must be checked in the options bar (the usual setting). If it's not checked, you must switch to the corresponding text layer using the Layers palette.

Transforming and Skewing Text

Start

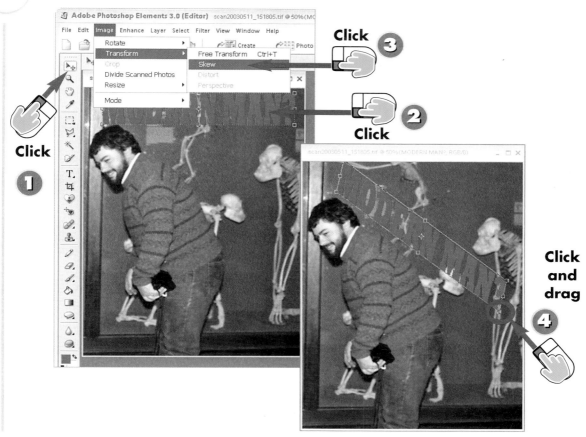

Click 3

Click 2

Click 1

Click and drag 4

End

1 Select the **Move** tool, or press **V**.

2 Click the text object you want to transform.

3 Choose **Image**, **Transform**, **Skew**.

4 Click and drag a handle of the selection box to resize and/or distort the text.

TIP

Grow or Distort Text
You can grow or distort text using the same procedure, except choose **Image**, **Transform**, **Free Transform** (or press **Ctrl+T**) in step 3. Try it and notice how this type of transformation differs from Skew.

HINT

Auto Select Layer
For step 2 to work, the Auto Select Layer box must be checked in the options bar (the usual setting). If it's not checked, you must switch to the corresponding text layer using the Layers palette.

Warping Text

Start

Click
2

Click
3

Click
1

1 Select the **Horizontal Type** tool.

2 Click the text you want to warp.

3 In the options bar, click the **Create Warped Text** button.

You can apply all kinds of fancy effects to text by this method, which is great for adding dramatic or comic touches to titles of albums and slideshows.

HINT

Auto Select Layer
For step 2 to work, the Auto Select Layer box must be checked in the options bar (the usual setting). If it's not checked, you must switch to the corresponding text layer using the Layers palette.

Click ④

Click ⑦

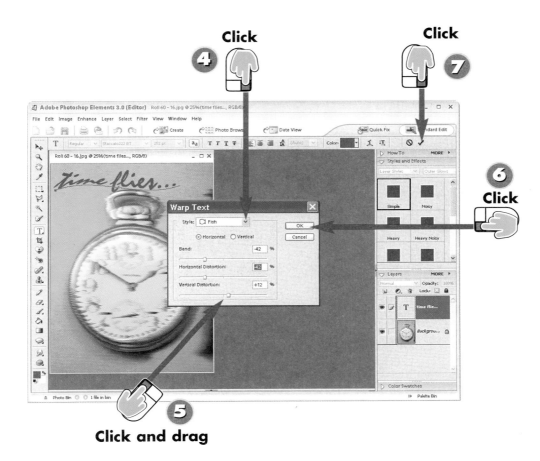

Click ⑥

Click and drag ⑤

④ Select a style from the drop-down menu, such as **Fish**.

⑤ Click and drag one or more sliders to adjust the degree of the effect.

⑥ Click **OK**.

⑦ Click the **Commit** button in the Options bar.

End

TIP

Another Way to Warp
Here's an alternative method for warping your words: Right-click the text and select **Warp Text** from the pop-up menu.

HINT

Warped, Not Crazy
Warping text is usually done for comic effect. For best results, choose a font with fat letters. Some fonts don't warp well. For example, Old English and cursive fonts can become downright unreadable.

Adding a Talk Bubble

Start

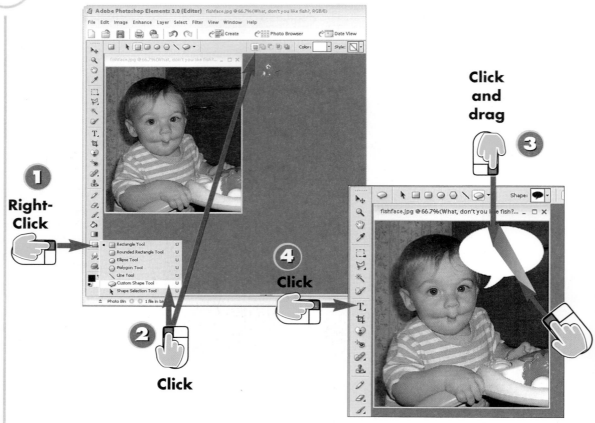

1 Right-click the **Rectangle** tool.

2 Select **Custom Shape Tool** and select **white** from the Color drop-down menu in the Options bar.

3 Click and drag to size the shape in the image area.

4 Select the **Horizontal Type** tool.

Oh, those wacky relatives and the wild things they say! A *talk bubble* can add a whimsical touch to your greeting cards and Webmail. It's actually just one of many shapes that Photoshop Elements can draw so that you don't have to create them free-hand.

TIP

Hearts and Flowers
The talk bubble—or *speech balloon*—is just one of an assortment of custom shapes. To pick one, after selecting the Custom Shape tool, select the **Shape** drop-down menu in the options bar.

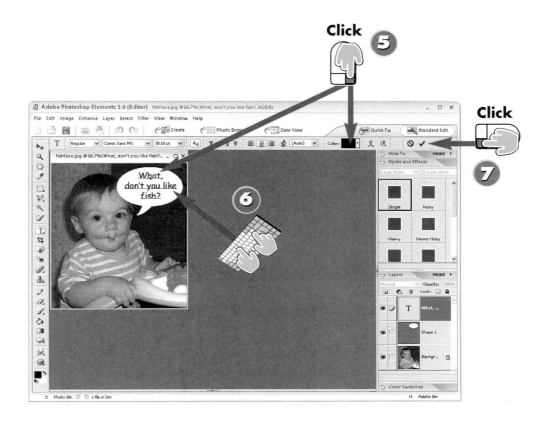

Click 5

Click 7

6

5 Select **black** from the Color drop-down menu in the Options bar.

6 Click inside the talk bubble and type some text.

7 Click the **Commit** button in the options bar.

End

Don't See a Talk Bubble?
The toolbar shows the Custom Shape tool you used last. If the Talk Bubble isn't there, select the Custom Shape tool and choose the shape you want from the Shape box in the options bar.

Other Shape Tools
Besides custom shapes, other tools in the Shape submenu in the toolbar are Rectangle, Rounded Rectangle, Ellipse, Polygon, and Line.

Applying a Text Effect

Start

Click

2

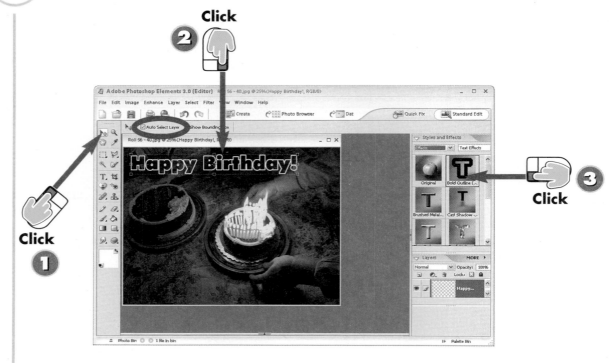

Click

1

Click

3

1 Select the **Move** tool, or press **V**.

2 Click the text that needs the effect (Auto Select Layer must be checked).

3 In the Effects palette, select the effect you want, such as **Bold Outline**, and click **Apply**.

End

Thumbnails in the Effects palette marked ABC are text effects, which you can apply to selected text with a click. If Photoshop Elements didn't include these "canned" effects, you'd have to be a skilled graphic artist, and it would take a lot more work to reproduce them.

TIP

Effects Palette Open?
To clear your work area, you may want to close or dock the Effects palette when you're finished. If it's not in the palette well, you can always get it back by choosing **Window**, **Effects**.

HINT

Applying Text Effects
Use only effects marked ABC. The others will affect the entire image, not just text. You can also apply text effects by dragging an effect from the palette and dropping it on the text.

Adding a Drop Shadow to Text

Start

Click

Click

Click

Click

1. Select the **Move** tool, or press **V**.

2. Click the text to which the drop shadow will be added (Auto Select Layer must be checked).

3. From the Style palette Libraries drop-down menu, select **Drop Shadows**.

4. Select a drop-shadow effect, such as **Hard Edge**.

End

INTRODUCTION
Place a drop shadow behind text to make it appear to "pop" out from the background so that it's more readable. This is particularly handy when the background has both light and dark areas and you can't find a solid area to serve as a background for the text that gives enough contrast.

HINT
Auto Select Layer
For step 2 to work, the Auto Select Layer box must be checked in the Options bar (the usual setting). If it's not checked, you must switch to the corresponding text layer using the Layers palette.

HINT
Make Your Own?
You can experiment with creating your own drop shadow effects if you know this: A drop shadow is actually a duplicate of the text object, in a contrasting color, positioned behind it and offset slightly.

Creating "Hollow" Text

Start

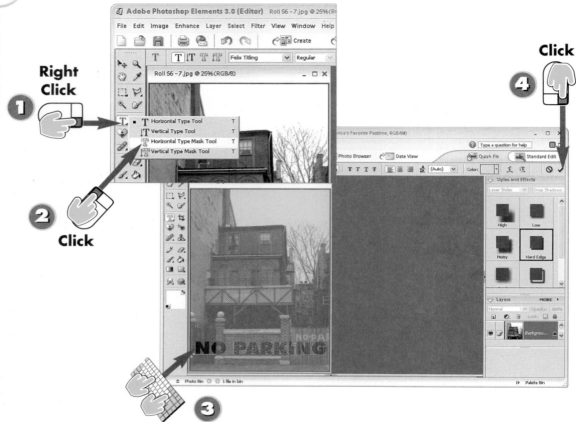

Right Click

①

②

Click

Click

④

③

1. Right-click the **Type** tool.

2. Select **Horizontal Type Mask Tool**.

3. Click the starting point of the text in the image. Type some text.

4. Click the **Commit** button in the Options bar.

A type mask is a selection—just like one you'd make with the Lasso, Marquee, or Magic Wand tool—but it's shaped like type. You can use it to fill type with pieces of the image (or another image).

TIP

Use Fat Letters

A type mask works best with big, fat letters. Use it on titles for a decorative effect. If you apply it to smaller text or to a block of words, the result probably won't be readable.

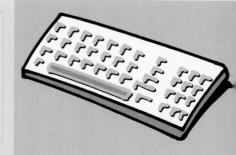

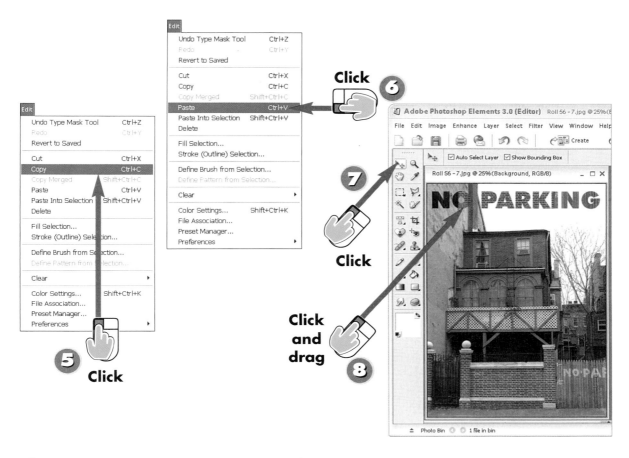

5 Choose **Edit**, **Copy**, or press **Ctrl+C**.

6 Choose **Edit**, **Paste**, or press **Ctrl+V**.

7 Select the **Move** tool, or press **V**.

8 Click and drag the copy of the masked text to reposition it in the image. The background from the original position shows through the hollow text.

End

Use a Variegated Background
This effect works best on variegated backgrounds, cutting and pasting from a lighter to a darker area, or vice versa. If the background is too uniform, the effect won't be obvious.

Take It Easy
Because they're selections, rather than actual objects, type masks aren't editable after you create them. Be careful to get their font, size, position, and (of course) spelling just the way you want it because you can't go back and fix it later.

Creating Snazzy Effects

With the invention of the electronic calculator, schoolchildren are the only ones who fret over doing arithmetic by hand. Similarly, you might be surprised at how many commercial artists don't draw from scratch anymore. Many of them earn their daily bread using computer graphics software like Photoshop Elements to make photos *look* like fine art.

When you've worked through the tasks in this part, you'll know many of their secrets. You can make greeting cards and party invitations look as if they were hand-drawn by a skilled sketch artist, create photo-realistic illustrations for flyers and newsletters, and add expensive-looking graphics that will give a professional touch to your personal Web site.

Photoshop Elements helps you achieve artistic effects by way of *filters* that can transform an image with a click, but in complex ways. The program comes with a wide variety of filters, and you can download even more of them (called *plug-ins*) from **www.adobe.com** and other vendors' Web sites. There are far too many filters to cover them all here, but you'll see enough to show you how easy they are to apply—and to start you thinking about all the creative possibilities.

How Did You Do *That?*

Before It helps to start with a photo that has an interesting composition, and some bright colors and contrasts.

After Here's some "fine art" that took less than a minute to make. It's the result of adding both the Palette Knife artistic filter and a Sandstone texture, and finally adjusting Hue for brighter greenery.

Adding a Decorative Border

Start

Click ①

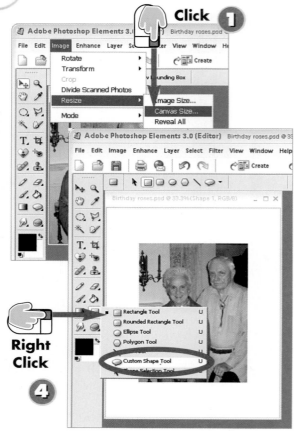

Right Click

④

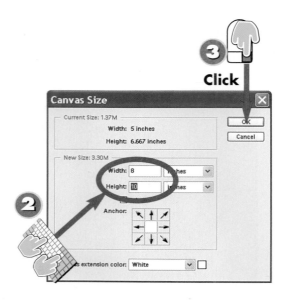

Click ③

②

① With a picture in the active image area, choose **Image**, **Resize**, **Canvas Size**.

② Type a Width the same as the print size and about 2 inches wider than the current image size. Do the same for Height.

③ Click **OK**.

④ Right-click the **Shape** tool in the toolbar and select **Custom Shape Tool**.

HINT

Know the Image Size
In this example, the image size of the photo is about 5×7 inches. Placing it on an 8×10 canvas adds just the right amount of border for the decorative frame.

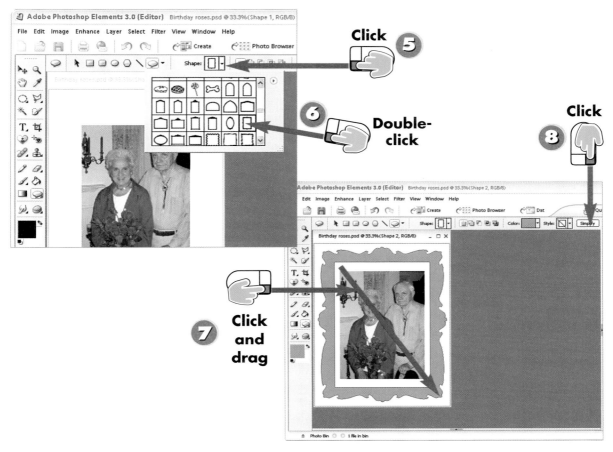

5️⃣ In the Options bar, open the **Shape** drop-down menu.

6️⃣ Double-click any **Frame** shape.

7️⃣ Click and drag in the image to surround the photo with the frame.

8️⃣ Click the **Simplify** button.

See next page

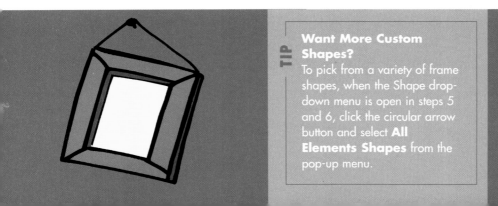

TIP

Want More Custom Shapes?
To pick from a variety of frame shapes, when the Shape drop-down menu is open in steps 5 and 6, click the circular arrow button and select **All Elements Shapes** from the pop-up menu.

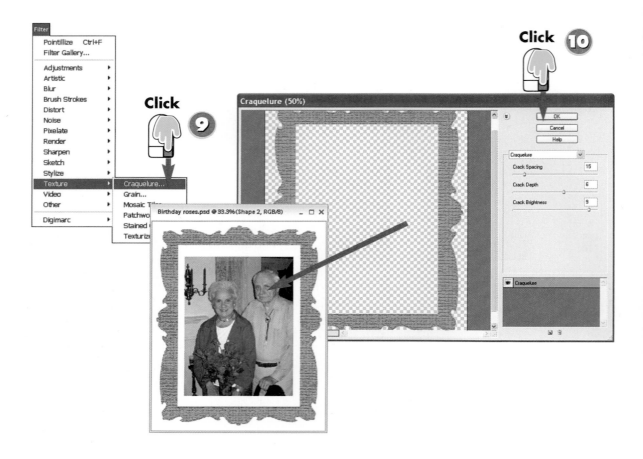

9 Choose **Filter**, **Texture**, **Craquelure**.

10 Click **OK**.

End

INTRODUCTION

The frame used here is just one of many Custom Shapes, which are ready-made so you don't have to do any freehand drawing. Categories include Animals, Arrows, Banners and Awards, Characters, Default, Frames, Fruit, Music, Nature, Objects, Ornaments, Shapes, Signs, Symbols, Talk Bubbles, and Tiles.

TIP

Craquelure Not Your Style?
Instead of applying the Craquelure filter in step 9, try any other effect or combination of effects from the **Filter** menu.

TIP

Don't See the Preview?
For the preview of the whole frame to be visible in the Craquelure dialog box in step 10, click the – button several times to reduce the view percentage from 100 to 14 percent.

Creating a Gradient Fill

Start

Click

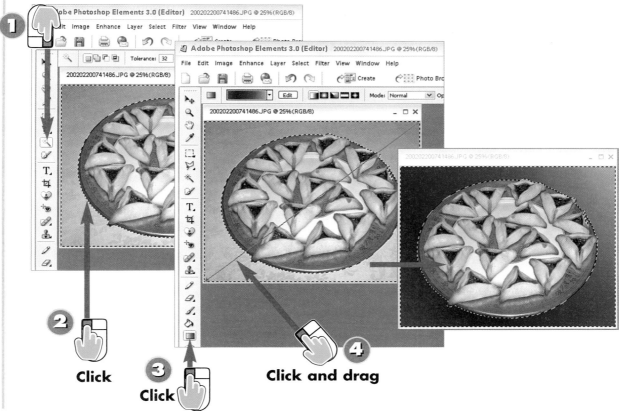

Click

Click

Click and drag

1. With the picture in the active image area, select the **Magic Wand** tool, or press **W**.

2. Click to select the area in the image to which the effect will be applied.

3. Select the **Gradient** tool, or press **G**.

4. Click and drag across the area to be filled in the direction you want the color gradation to take. (Press **Ctrl+D** to release the selection.)

End

A *gradient fill* is a blended transition—usually between two colors—within a selected area. In this example, the gradient is applied to the entire background, but it could also be used to fill any object you select, even hollow text.

Making Your Selection
Use any combination of selection tools in step 1 (Magic Wand, Lassos, or Marquees). Press **Shift** as you select with a tool to add an area to the current selection, **Alt** to subtract.

Mix Your Own Gradients
After selecting the Gradient tool, clicking the **Edit** button in the Options bar opens the Gradient Editor, which contains options for creating custom gradients.

Mounting a Photo on a Fancy Background

Start

Click ❶

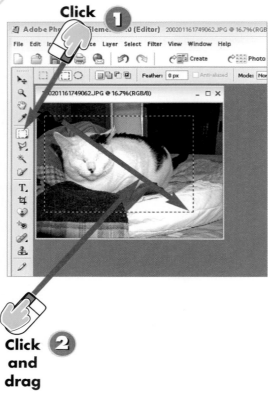

Click ❸

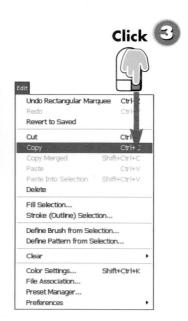

Click ❷
and
drag

❶ With the photo open in the active image window, select the **Rectangular Marquee** tool, or press **M**.

❷ Click and drag to frame the image.

❸ Choose **Edit**, **Copy**, or press **Ctrl+C**.

INTRODUCTION

Putting a cherished family photo in an expensive frame is a fine idea, but the price of a custom matte is a needless expense. Create your own fancy background, and it won't cost you any more than a little extra printer ink. And yours will probably be prettier than any you can buy.

HINT

Crop, While You're at It
You don't need to crop your photo first, because selecting the area to copy has the same result. But if the selection is too small in relation to the fancy background image, resample the image first to increase resolution.

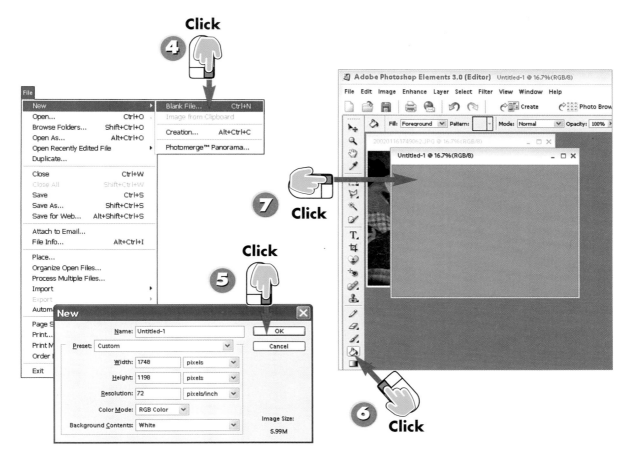

4 Choose **File**, **New**, **Blank File** or press **Ctrl+N**.

5 Increase the Width and Height measurements by about 20%; then click **OK**.

6 Select the **Paint Bucket** tool, or press **K**.

7 Click in the new image area to fill it with color.

See next page

TIP

What Color Do You Prefer?
The Paint Bucket tool deposits the currently selected foreground color. To make a different choice, click the topmost color patch at the bottom of the toolbar, and make a new selection from the Color Picker.

TIP

You're Not Stuck
In step 6, for a different look, after selecting the **Paint Bucket** tool, choose **Pattern** in the Fill box in the Options bar, select a pattern, and click inside the image area to fill the background with the pattern.

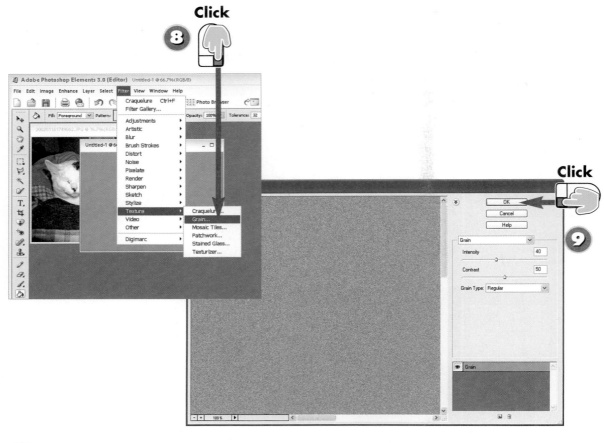

8 Choose **Filter**, **Texture**, **Grain**.

9 Click **OK**.

By adding a frame using Photoshop Elements, you can begin to think of every photo you shoot as just the starting point for a piece of attractive, personalized artwork. Traditionally, film photographers didn't get involved in such artistic cutting and pasting, but in today's digital realm, it's just so easy.

Varying Textures
Like the Craquelure filter shown previously, you can vary Grain by adjusting sliders after step 8. Other available textures are Mosaic Tiles, Patchwork, Stained Glass, and Texturizer (for surface effects such as Canvas and Burlap).

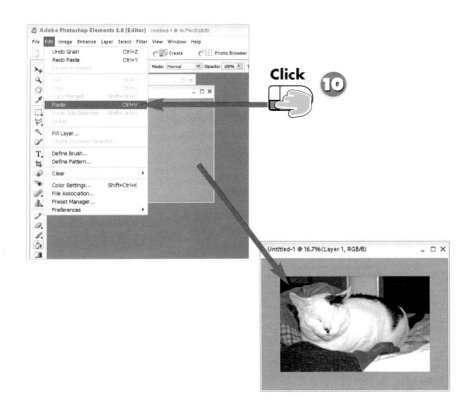

(10) Choose **Edit**, **Paste** from the menu bar, or press **Ctrl+V**.

End

Metal or Paper?
Applying a gradient effect to the background instead of the grainy texture can give the impression of a metallic picture frame.

Didn't Work as Advertised?
The size of the pasted photo in the new window depends on the relative image sizes of the two pictures. If the photo size needs adjustment, select the **Move** tool after step 9 and reposition/resize it.

Adding a Beautiful Sky

Start

Click

1

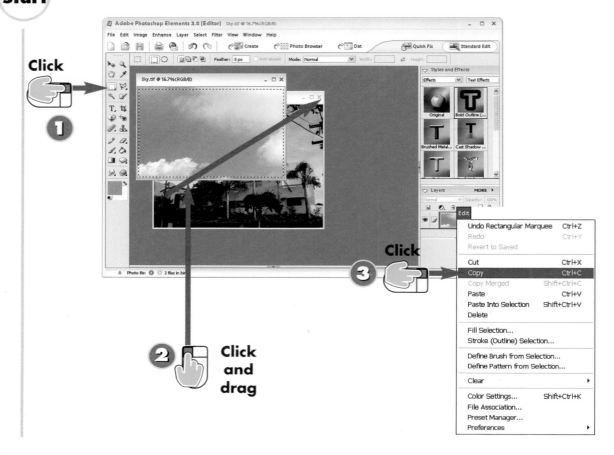

Click

3

2 **Click and drag**

1. Start with two images open: a pretty sky and a scene with sky you want to replace. Select the **Rectangular Marquee** tool.

2. Click and drag in the pretty sky window to select a large rectangular piece.

3. Choose **Edit**, **Copy**, or press **Ctrl+C**.

TIP

Be Sure to Grab It All
In step 2, use any combination of selection tools. The Lasso tool is particularly handy for irregular areas, followed by several Shift-clicks with **Magic Wand** to get the rest.

4 Select the **Magic Wand** tool, or press **W**.

5 In the scene window, click to select the sky that needs replacing. (Shift+click to add other areas to the selection.)

6 Choose **Edit**, **Paste into Selection**, or press **Shift+Ctrl+V**.

TIP
Release and Let's Go
When you're finished with this task, to release the selection and continue working, choose **Select**, **Deselect**, or press **Ctrl+D**.

HINT
But Don't Leave Home
You can try the same technique used here for replacing sky to replace the background of any photo with any other shot. Keep your subjects in place and take them to some exotic locale—at no expense!

Creating a High-Contrast Black-and-White Picture

Start

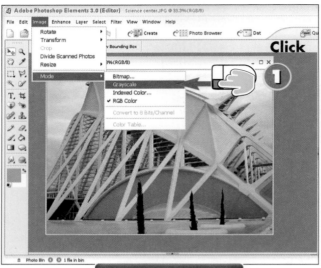

Click

1

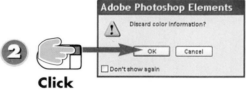

2 **Click**

Click

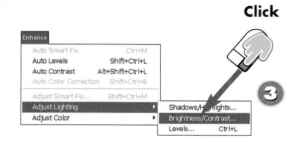

3

1 With a picture in the active image area, choose **Image**, **Mode**, **Grayscale**.

2 Click **OK**.

3 Choose **Enhance**, **Adjust Lighting**, **Brightness/Contrast**.

Back in the ancient days of film, high-contrast (hi-con) transparencies were called *Kodaliths*, the name of a Kodak product for mastering printing plates. You can create some dramatic artistic effects doing the same thing digitally—by converting a photo to black-and-white, with no shading.

Don't Do This to Your Boss

Hi-con doesn't make flattering portraits. Clean-shaven men with five o'clock shadow end up with real stubble trouble, and wispy laugh lines become deep trenches.

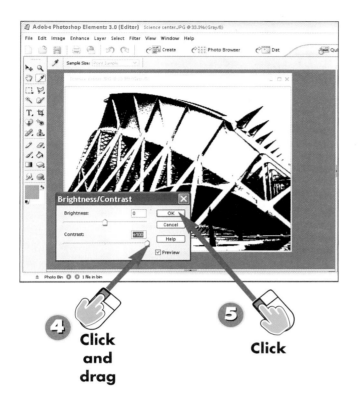

Click and drag **Click**

4 Adjust the **Contrast** slider to **100**.

5 Click **OK**.

End

Adjust Brightness
In step 4, after increasing Contrast, it may also be necessary to adjust the Brightness slider a bit, as done here.

Consider the Source
Hi-con effects work best on images with smooth surfaces and sharp edges, such as architectural views. If the source photo has shaded areas, keep the Contrast setting below 80 percent to preserve some grayscale.

Making a Photo Look Like an Oil Painting

Start

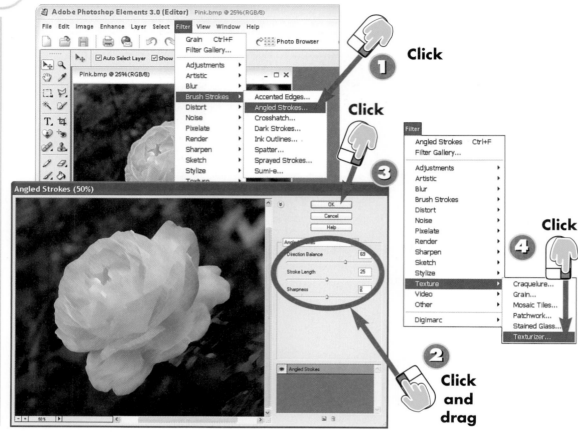

Click

Click

Click

Click and drag

1 With a photo in the active image area, choose **Filter**, **Brush Strokes**, **Angled Strokes**.

2 Optionally, adjust the **Direction Balance**, **Stroke Length**, and **Sharpness** sliders.

3 When you see the desired effect in the Preview window, click **OK**.

4 Choose **Filter**, **Texture**, **Texturizer**.

INTRODUCTION

No one's proposing you start cranking out fake Rembrandts, but there's something about brushstrokes on canvas that says high class. Try this with the family portrait and pretend you sat for a Dutch master.

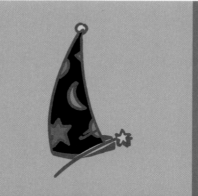

Tuning Your Strokes

HINT

The slider options in step 2 control the magnitude of the effect. You want to balance making the brushstrokes obvious enough to be seen, yet not so much as to obliterate fine detail in the picture.

5 In the Texture box, select **Canvas**.

6 Click **OK**.

How Rough Is Your Canvas?
As with brushstrokes, you can adjust Texturizer options to control roughness and lighting on the canvas: Scaling, Relief, and Light Direction. The Invert option reverses light and dark effects.

No Rules
There are no rules for applying artistic effects. Be guided by your own taste. For example, instead of a Canvas texture, try Burlap or Sandstone. And remember, results vary depending on the source material.

Posterizing a Picture

Start

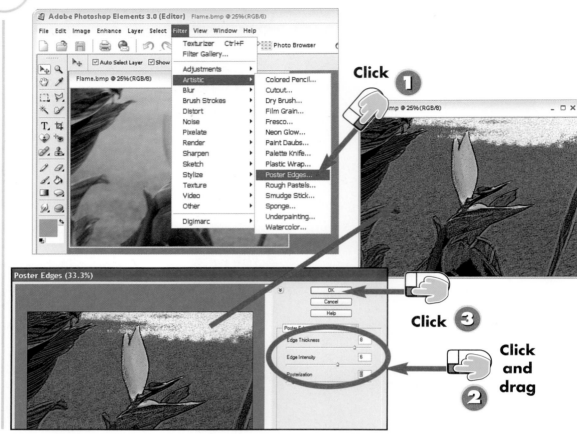

Click 1

Click 3

Click and drag 2

1 With a picture in the active image area, choose **Filter**, **Artistic**, **Poster Edges**.

2 Optionally, adjust sliders for **Edge Thickness**, **Edge Intensity**, and **Posterization**.

3 Click **OK**.

End

Posterization became popular in the psychedelic movement of the 1960s as a way of making images seem more intense. Photoshop Elements includes a filter called Poster Edges to create this effect.

HINT
Ideas for Greeting Cards?
Applying the Poster Edges effect to a photo can make it look like a fine watercolor and ink drawing, or an elaborate illustration in a children's book.

Making a Photo Look Like a Sketch

Start

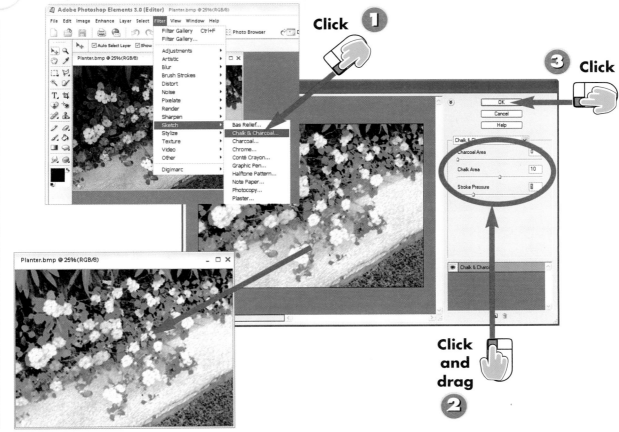

Click 1

3 Click

Click and drag 2

1. With a photo in the active image area, choose **Filter**, **Sketch**, **Chalk & Charcoal**.

2. Optionally, adjust sliders for **Charcoal Area**, **Chalk Area**, and **Stroke Pressure**.

3. Click **OK**.

End

INTRODUCTION

Whether your drawings look like stick figures or you're just in too big a hurry to sit down with your sketchpad, Photoshop Elements can make any photo look hand-drawn. For example, take a photo of the curbside view of your home, convert it to a sketch, and use it to illustrate personalized party invitations or stationery.

HINT

Make It Snappy
Although level correction isn't a required step, it's applied to this example to darken the lines so that the result reproduces better in print.

Applying the Pointillize Filter

Start

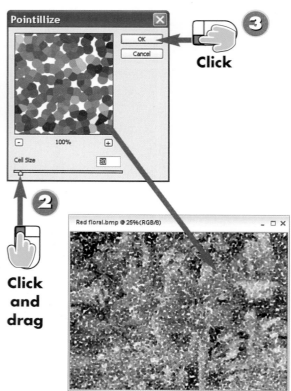

Click

Click

**Click
and
drag**

1 With a photo in the active image area, choose **Filter**, **Pixelate**, **Pointillize**.

2 Optionally, adjust the **Cell Size** slider to get the look you want.

3 Click **OK**.

End

Pointillism is a technique pioneered by French Impressionist painter Georges Seurat more than a century ago. His paintings are composed of thousands of tiny dots of bright colors—and the overall effect was apparent only when viewing the work from a distance. In a sense, he invented pixels, which are the building blocks of today's computerized, digital images.

TIP

How Big Is a Cell?
Cell size in step 2 controls the size of the picture dots and the magnitude of the effect. You want it large enough to make the effect visible, small enough to preserve important picture details.

Adding a Motion Blur

Start

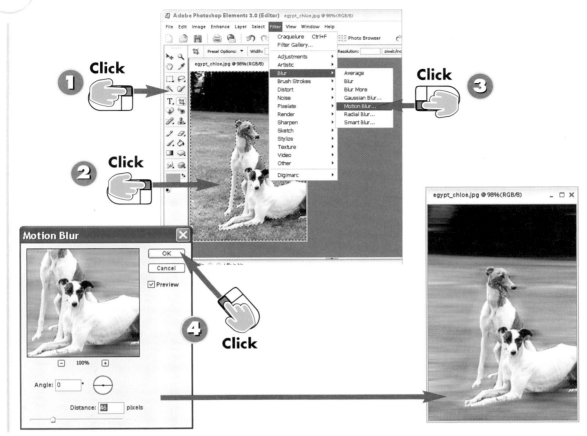

Click ①

Click ②

Click ③

Motion Blur

④ **Click**

1 With a photo in the active image area, click a selection tool, such as **Magic Wand**.

2 Click to select the area in the image to which you want the blurring effect applied.

3 Choose **Filter**, **Blur**, **Motion Blur**.

4 Click **OK**. (To keep working on the photo, press **Ctrl+D** to release your selection.)

End

INTRODUCTION

Many of the artistic filters in Photoshop Elements might well be applied to the whole picture. Blurring is an example of a filter you'd normally apply only to a selected portion of an image, such as the propeller of this aircraft replica.

TIP

Giving Directions
Change the angle of the blur to change the direction of the perceived motion. This horizontal blur brings to mind the cross-country speed of greyhounds, but a vertical or steeply angled blur might imply the dogs were taking off into space.

Blurring an Image All Over

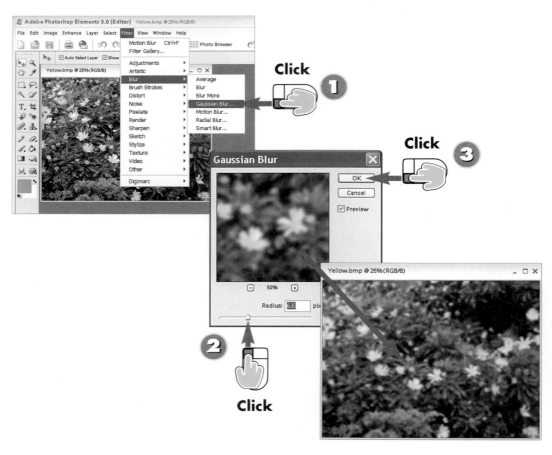

Click ①

Click ③

② **Click**

End

① With a photo in the active image area, select **Filter**, **Blur**, **Gaussian Blur**.

② Optionally, drag the **Radius** slider to make the picture more or less blurry.

③ Click **OK**.

Putting a Photo Behind Glass

Start

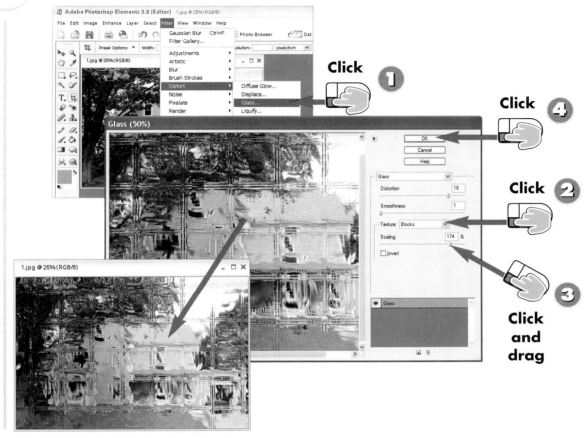

Click 1

Click 4

Click 2

Click and drag 3

1. With a photo in the active image area, select **Filter**, **Distort**, **Glass**.

2. Select a glass texture, such as **Blocks**.

3. Optionally, drag the **Scaling** slider to change the size of the blocks.

4. Click **OK**.

End

INTRODUCTION

Use the Glass filter to give a photo a little *trompe-l'oeil* flair; somehow, adding a layer of glass in front of the picture makes it look that much more real—as though the printed page or monitor screen is actually a window.

HINT

It'll Really Frost You
If you're looking for an arty, painted appearance and haven't gotten the results you want using other filters, try a careful application of the Glass filter using the Frosted glass texture. You'll be surprised at the organic effects you get.

TIP

Honey, I Shrunk the Photo
A similar effect is Plastic Wrap (select **Filter**, **Artistic**, **Plastic Wrap**). Using this filter, you can make the subject of your photo look as though it has been shrink-wrapped with a clear film.

Trimming a Photo into a Custom Shape

Start

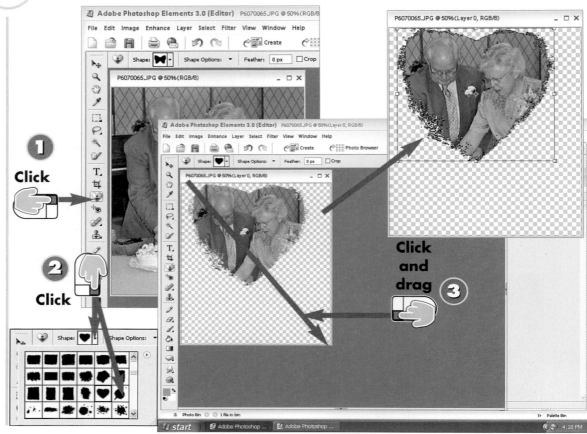

1 Click

2 Click

3 Click and drag

① Select the **Cookie Cutter** tool from the toolbox.

② Click to open the **Shape** drop-down menu, and then select a shape.

③ Click and drag in the document window to create the shape.

End

HINT
Cutting and Cropping
After you've applied the Cookie Cutter tool to your image, you might want to use the Crop tool to get rid of the extra empty space surrounding the new shape.

HINT
There's Time to Get It Right
Until you press Enter, click the Commit button on the options bar, or switch to another tool or layer, you can move and resize the shape as much as you want to perfectly frame your picture.

Shining a Spotlight on Your Subject

Start

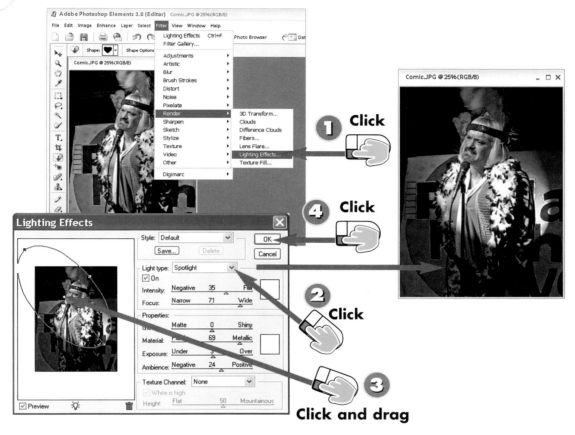

End

1. With a photo in the active image area, select **Filter**, **Render**, **Lighting Effects**.

2. Select a **Light Type**, such as **Spotlight**.

3. Drag the light so that it shines on the subject of the photo.

4. Click **OK**.

Painting and Drawing

Many people think of Photoshop Elements mainly as a digital photo lab, but it's also an art studio. So, welcome to your all-electronic work-and-play room—where you never have to wear a smock, clean a brush, or deal with that nasty turpentine.

Those of you who start with a photo as a background may have a more practical purpose in mind—such as making ads and brochures.

And along with adding text, combining your photos with your original artwork gives a wonderfully personal touch. Recipients of your greeting cards, party invitations, photo email, and newsletters will appreciate the care you took—even though none of this is nearly as hard as they might imagine!

Getting a bit more serious, you can also illustrate business presentations, school reports, and instructional materials with professional-looking diagrams and drawings. No more crude pencil sketches, and good-bye forever to stick figures!

But don't stop there. Set aside a rainy Saturday afternoon to discover the joy of digital painting and drawing. Vincent Van Gogh never had such a rich and varied set of tools!

Look What I Made!

Paint and draw over a photo to create your own custom graphics for postcards.

Or just paint and draw from scratch for the pure joy of it!

Creating a Shape

Start

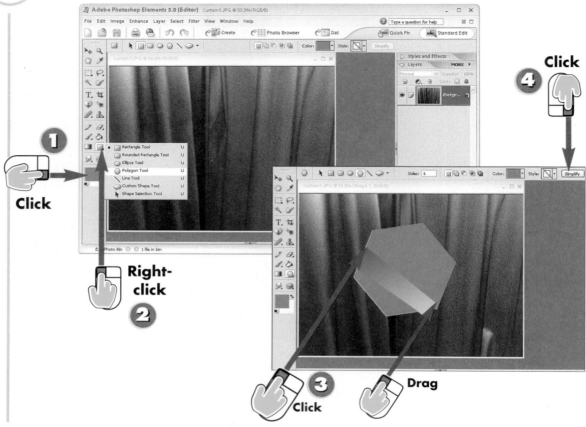

Click ①

Right-click ②

Click ③

Drag

Click ④

① Click to select a foreground color.

② Right-click the **Shape** tool and select the shape tool you want, such as **Polygon Tool**.

③ Click and drag in the image area to adjust the size and proportions of the shape.

④ To make the pixels of the shape editable, click the **Simplify** button.

End

TIP

Shift to Get Regular
Hold down the **Shift** key while you draw to make Rectangles square, Ellipses circular. Lines follow the closest 45° angle.

HINT

Moving and Resizing
To move or resize a shape before it's simplified, use the Shape Selection tool. When simplified, use the Move tool instead. For best-quality shapes, always try to resize before you simplify.

Adding a Bevel to a Shape

1 Click

2 Click

3 Double-click

1 With a shape selected, select **Layer Styles** from the **Styles and Effects** palette's drop-down menu.

2 Select **Bevels** in the Style Libraries drop-down menu.

3 Double-click the bevel style you want to apply.

End

INTRODUCTION

New shapes can look plain and flat. Adding a bevel gives the shape a dimensional quality that can also make it stand out from the background. Photoshop Elements provides a nice selection of bevel styles that can give your object a bold, dimensional look. Just click the one you like, and it's applied automatically.

TIP

Close It Quick!
If the palette is open but docked, as shown, click anywhere outside the palette to close it after step 3.

TIP

Selecting Shapes
If the shape you want isn't the most recent one you created, select it with the **Move** tool before you do step 1 (Auto Select Layer must be checked). If the shape is one of many on a layer, use the **Shape Selection** tool instead.

Filling a Shape with Color

Start

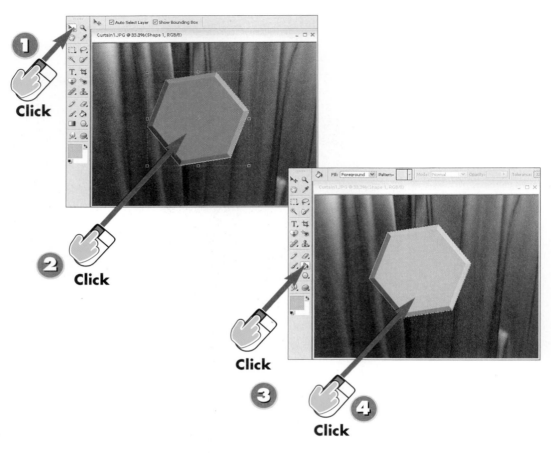

1 Click

2 Click

3 Click

4 Click

End

① Having chosen the foreground color, select the **Move** tool or press **V**. (Auto Select Layer must be checked.)

② Select the shape.

③ Select the **Paint Bucket** tool, or press **K**.

④ Click inside the shape to apply the color.

If you've worked through the tasks to this point, this won't be the first time you've used the Paint Bucket tool. But notice how quickly and easily you can recolor a shape. Always remember that the Paint Bucket—like other painting tools—uses whatever you've selected as the current foreground color.

TIP

Change the Fill Color
Before you do step 1, click the **Foreground** color swatch at the bottom of the toolbar and make a selection from the **Color Picker**.

TIP

Fill with a Pattern
If you prefer a pattern rather than a color, before doing step 2, select **Pattern** from the **Fill** drop-down menu in the Options bar; then make a selection from the **Pattern** menu.

Using the Eyedropper to Pick a Color

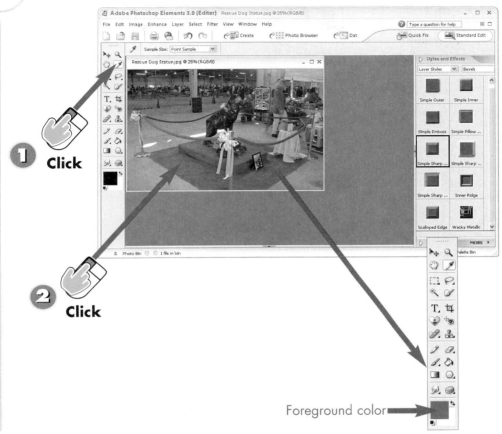

1 Click

2 Click

Foreground color

1 Select the **Eyedropper** tool, or press **I**.

2 Click a color you want to match in the image area. The foreground color changes to the color of your sample, and you can now use any tool that applies color.

INTRODUCTION

Want to pick a color for a new shape or brush stroke that exactly matches some color in the image? The Eyedropper tool sucks up the color you click and loads it as the current foreground color. Whatever painting or drawing tool you use next applies that color.

TIP

Changing Sample Size
Before step 2, you can choose **3 x 3 Average** or **5 x 5 Average** to set the number of pixels in the area the Eyedropper will sample. (Remember, it's an average, so the resulting color may be a blend of the sampled pixels.)

HINT

Whenever You See It
Photoshop Elements uses the Eyedropper pointer in other places, such as the Color Swatches palette, and it always works as a color selector.

Using the Color Swatches Palette

Click ①

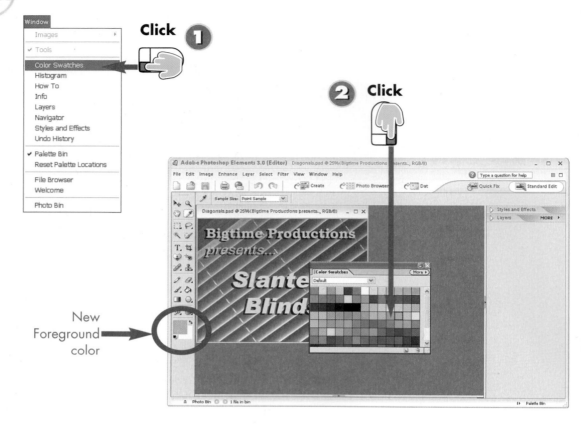

Click ②

New Foreground color

① Choose **Window**, **Color Swatches**.

② Click the color you want to use next. The foreground color changes to the color of your sample, and you are ready to use any tool that applies color.

End

Rolling Your Own

TIP

You can save your own favorite colors in the Swatches palette. To save the current foreground color, scroll down to the blank area at the bottom of the palette and click to add a swatch.

Painting and Drawing with a Brush and Pencil

Start

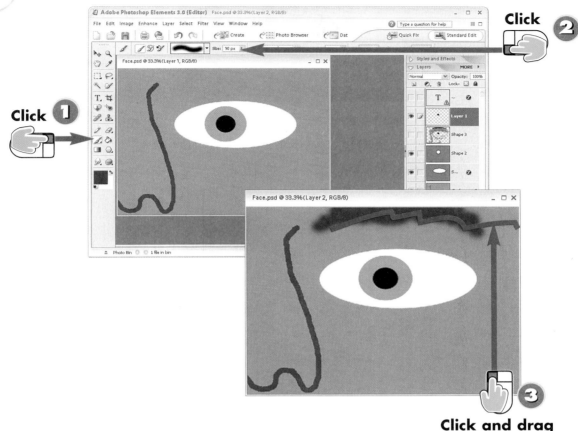

Click 1

Click 2

Click and drag 3

1. Select the **Brush** tool.

2. Set brush properties in the options bar, such as **Size**.

3. Click and drag in the image area to apply each brush stroke.

End

INTRODUCTION

Use the Brush tool to do freehand painting (or Impressionist Brush to paint over and blur). The Pencil tool right beside it in the toolbar works much the same, except pencil lines don't have soft edges.

HINT

Brush Stroke Technique

Keep holding down the mouse button and paint with a scrubbing motion to apply a single, continuous brush stroke. Or, click and release the mouse button frequently as you paint to apply dabs of color.

TIP

A Tip on Brush Tips

Select the tip size and brush stroke properties in the options bar before you do step 2. Pick one of the preset brushes or adjust the other options to create your own.

Controlling How Brushes Behave

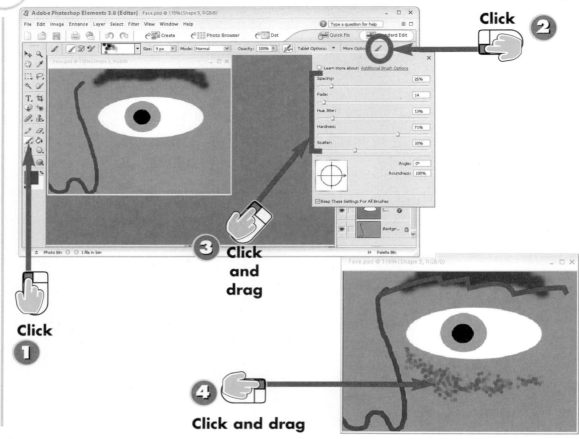

Click ①

Click ②

Click and drag ③

Click and drag ④

1. Select the **Brush** tool.

2. Click **More Options** in the options bar.

3. Adjust how the brush works by dragging a slider or typing a new percentage for one or more options.

4. Click and drag in the image area to apply each brush stroke.

End

If you really want to get arty with brush tips, you can make all kinds of adjustments in the options bar, before you start painting. Also located there is the Airbrush button, which generates a spray of pixels at the brush tip. (Access the full range of options from the More Options drop-down menu.)

HINT

Lots to Choose From
There are more than a dozen categories of preset brushes in the options bar, and you have the choice of fine-tuning any of them by making adjustments using the More Options drop-down menu.

TIP

Still More Options
In the options bar, Mode controls effects for artistic purposes, as well as for doing fine photo retouching. Opacity, in effect, is paint thickness—lower numbers are more like watercolor.

Painting with the Pattern Stamp

Start

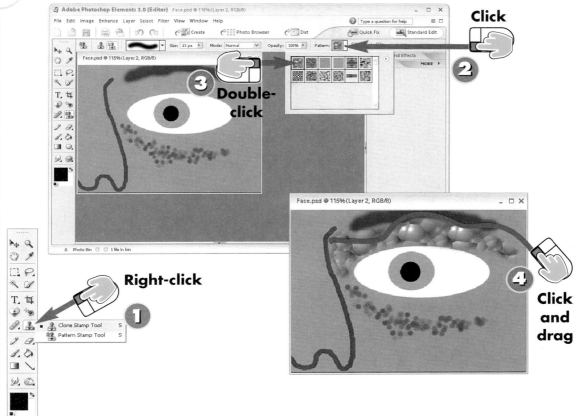

Click

Right-click

Double-click

Click and drag

1. Right-click the **Stamp** tool and select **Pattern Stamp Tool**.

2. Open the **Pattern** menu in the options bar.

3. Double-click to select a pattern from the Pattern drop-down menu.

4. Click and drag in the image area to paint, just as you would with the Brush tool.

End

INTRODUCTION

Painting with a pattern is lots of fun—and something you can't do nearly as easily with physical paint and paper. The result is more like making cutouts of wallpaper or fabric and pasting them down—much like art techniques collage and mixed media.

HINT

The Other Stamp Tool
The Pattern Stamp's roommate in the toolbar, the Clone Stamp, isn't so much for painting as it is a tool for removing unwanted details, such as facial blemishes, from photos.

HINT

Options, Options
Notice that there are all kinds of choices in the options bar. Make your selections before doing step 2, just as you would with a brush.

Using the Erasers

Start

Click
2

Click
1

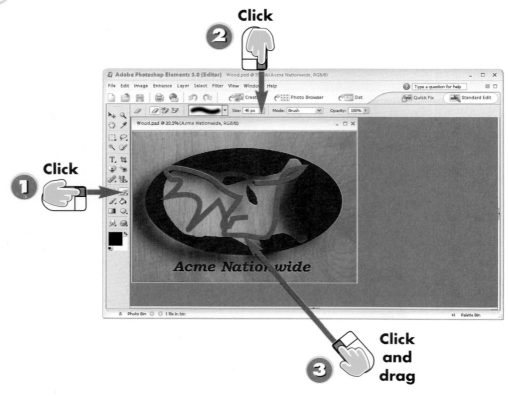

Click and drag
3

1. Select the **Eraser** tool, or press **E**.

2. If you want, change the tool properties in the options bar.

3. Click and drag over the pixels you want to erase.

End

The Eraser tool works just like a brush—but removes pixels in its path rather than depositing them. It only affects shapes on the layer currently selected, so you may want to open the Layers palette first to get your bearings.

Undo Instead?
Use the Eraser tool for partial erasures of shapes. To simply get rid of painting mistakes, **Edit**, **Undo** or **Edit**, **Step Backward** may be faster and cleaner.

Other Eraser Tools
Right-click in step 1 to select **Background Eraser**, which deletes a single color sampled from the center of a brush, or **Magic Eraser**, which deletes areas of similar-colored pixels with a click (like Magic Wand does for selections).

Softening Edges

Start

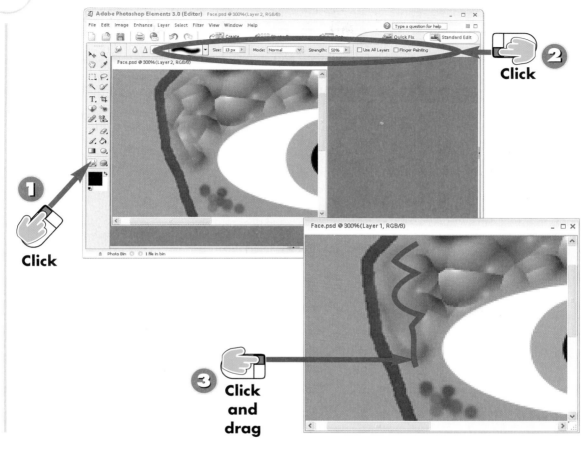

2 **Click**

1 **Click**

3 **Click and drag**

1 With the edge you want to soften zoomed in the image area, select the **Smudge** tool or press **F**.

2 If you want, change the tool properties in the options bar.

3 Click and drag along the edge to soften it.

End

Some of the painting tools can be used either for painting or for retouching details in photos, and the Smudge tool is one of these. Artists who've worked with pastels will be familiar with the technique of rubbing chalk edges to soften them.

Finger Paint, Oh Boy!
If you're tempted to make a creative mess the clean, electronic way, check the **Finger Paint** box in the options bar before you do step 2.

Impressionist Brush Instead?
The effect of the Smudge tool may be too subtle for your taste. For more pronounced blurring, use the Impressionist Brush tool in one of the smaller brush sizes. Also try effects in the Filter, Blur submenu.

Flattering Your Subjects

Okay, in other parts of this book we've talked about Photoshop Elements being your photo lab and your art studio—but why not also think of it as a one-stop health and beauty spa? Digital retouching, if not overdone, can perk up your friends and loved ones, making them appear to shed pounds, revitalizing their complexions, and putting that old sparkle in their eyes—all without risky fad diets, treatments, or pills!

But let's emphasize—*don't overdo it*. As a good rule of thumb, try to soften rather than erase. Leave some lines, freckles, and whatever other imperfections give your friend her unique character and winning charm. Go too far, and you'll have a slick beauty shot of a lifeless mannequin.

Many of the techniques described in this part were applied to the photo on the facing page. Retouching included correcting a color cast, softening facial lines with the Blur tool, removing a mole with the Spot Healing Brush tool, adding eyelight with the Brush tool, lightening shadows and darkening blown-out highlights with the Dodge and Burn tools, and intensifying lip and eye color with the Sponge tool set to Saturate.

The transformation took about 10 minutes—and it makes a lovely person even lovelier.

What a Difference a Pixel Makes!

Before

After

Adding Eyelight for Personality

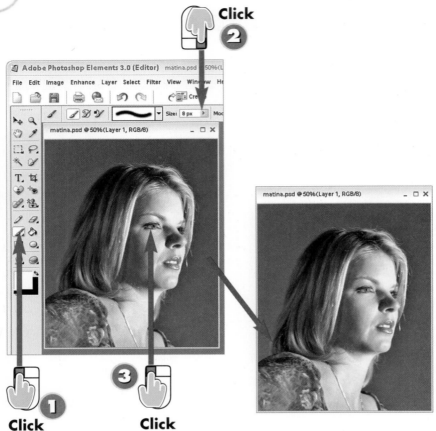

Start

Click 2

Click 1

Click 3

1. With white as the current foreground color, select the **Brush** tool.

2. In the options bar, select a brush tip smaller than the iris of the eye.

3. Click inside the eye lens, at the edge of the iris. (Repeat to match position in the other eye.)

End

INTRODUCTION

Eyelight is a trick of Hollywood cinematographers, who aim a small spotlight directly at the star's eyes to add sparkle. They don't give movie villains eyelight, and somehow you instinctively know they are shiftless, not to be trusted.

HINT

Eyelight Is a Reflection
Instead of being centered in the eye, the position of the eyelight should match the direction of the main light source (called *key light*). If the key is high and to the left, put the white dot in the top-left center of the eye.

HINT

Get It Right
Besides indicating the direction of the light source, the positions of the eyelights in each eye should match exactly. If not, your star could look either cross- or wall-eyed.

Fixing Dark and Light Areas in a Photo

Start

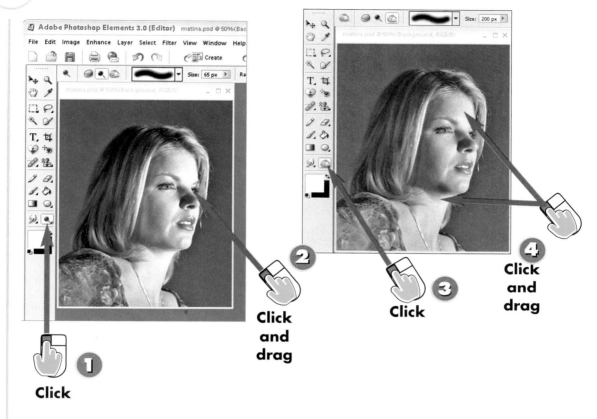

Click

**Click
and
drag**

Click

**Click
and
drag**

① With the photo in the active image area, select the **Dodge** tool, or press **O**.

② Click and drag to paint an area to recover detail from its shadows.

③ Select the **Burn** tool, or press **J**.

④ Click and drag to paint an area that needs detail recovered from its highlights.

End

INTRODUCTION

Dodge and Burn are *toning* tools with names carried over from traditional darkroom techniques for increasing or decreasing exposure in areas of shadow or highlight when printing film *negatives*. The Dodge tool lightens dark areas (overexposed), and the Burn tool darkens light areas (underexposed).

HINT

Crushed or Blown Out?
Dark areas that are totally black are said to be *crushed*, and totally white areas are *blown out*. Neither has any detail you can recover by using these steps. Try to light the shot better next time before you take it.

TIP

Dodge/Burn Options
Besides a selection of brush tips, the options bar contains settings for Mode (Shadows, Midtones, or Highlights) and Strength (similar to print light intensity in the darkroom).

Removing or Softening Facial Lines

Start

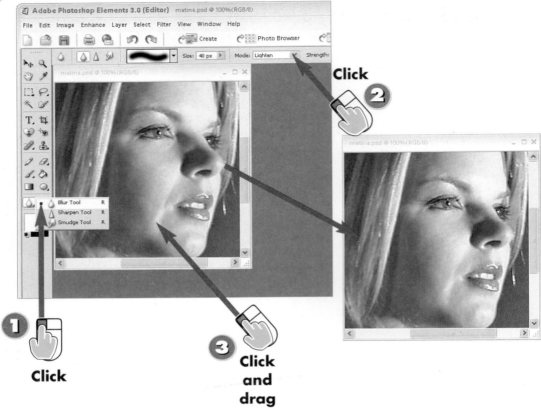

Click ②

Click ①

Click and drag ③

① With a zoomed photo in the active image area, select the **Blur** tool.

② In the options bar, select **Lighten** from the **Mode** drop-down menu.

③ Click and drag several times over a facial line to blend it away.

End

INTRODUCTION

This one's sure to please—the wrinkle remover. Remember, the lines in the face convey expressiveness, so don't paint them all out. Ask yourself: Are these crow's feet or laugh lines? (To work in even finer detail, you can use the Blur tool much the same way.)

HINT

Mode Options
The Blur tool can be versatile, depending on this setting. Besides Normal, Darken, and Lighten (used here), the effect can be confined to Hue, Saturation, Color, or Luminosity.

TIP

To Be Precise About It
For best results, pick a Soft Round brush tip in the options bar with a Size just slightly larger than the facial lines you're retouching—and trace along the line as you paint.

Removing Facial Blemishes

Start

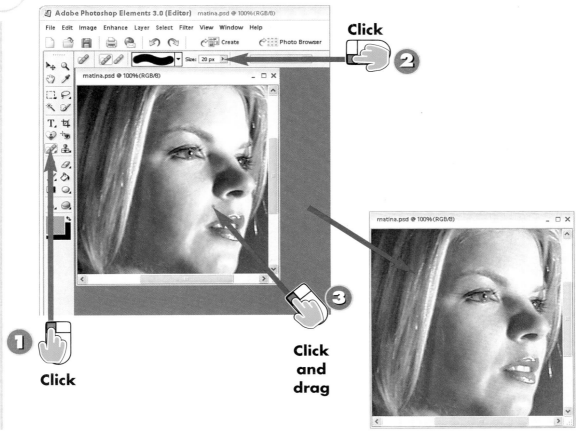

Click
2

Click
1

Click
and
drag
3

1 With a zoomed photo in the active image area, select the **Spot Healing Brush** tool or press **J**.

2 Choose a brush size just slightly larger than the blemish you want to erase.

3 Click once on the blemish to remove it.

End

That's right—the Spot Healing Brush tool is a painless zit zapper. But its marvels don't stop there. You can use it to cover up any part of a picture with textures Elements creates based on the surrounding pixels. Give it a try to get rid of spots on flower petals, lint on clothes, or any spot you can dab.

HINT

The Big Jobs
The Spot Healing Brush works best on, well, spots! Use it to retouch small, "clickable" objects surrounded by relatively clear, flat areas of color, such as moles, pimples, and dust motes. Often, you'll want to retouch larger areas and objects that are right next to other objects you don't want to affect, such as tattoos and smudges. For these jobs, try using the Healing Brush tool instead. Turn to "Painting Problem Areas Away," **p.130**, to learn more.

Changing Hair Color

Start

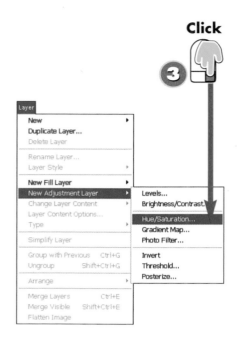

Click

3

Click

1

Click and drag

2

1 Select the **Lasso** tool, or press **L**.

2 Click and drag to trace the outline of the hair.

3 Choose **Layer**, **New Adjustment Layer**, **Hue/Saturation**.

INTRODUCTION

Being able to digitally recolor hair opens up all kinds of possibilities. Try on new looks and print them out to show the colorist at your hair salon. Change your Web photo because an ardent admirer has a thing for redheaded dudes. Or—go blue, pink, or green without fear of social stigma.

HINT

It's Cake, It's a Sandwich
There's a lot more about layers in a later part, but in these steps you're creating a special layer to contain just the Hue/Saturation effect. This adjustment layer doesn't contain any part of the image. By selecting the area you want to modify before creating the adjustment layer, you restrict its effects to that area.

Click 4

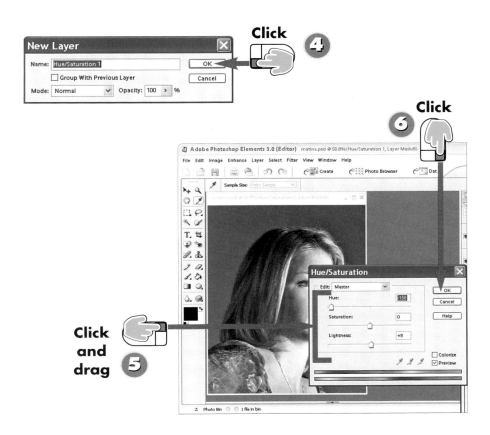

Click 6

Click and drag 5

4 Click **OK**.

5 Adjust sliders to change the hair color.

6 Click **OK**.

End

Want Subtler Color?
To soften the effect of the Hue/Saturation layer on the underlying hair color, decrease the value of **Opacity** for the new layer in the Layers palette.

Keep Those Layers
To keep a version of the image that contains editable layers, save your file as a Photoshop (**.psd**) file.

Painting Problem Areas Away

Start

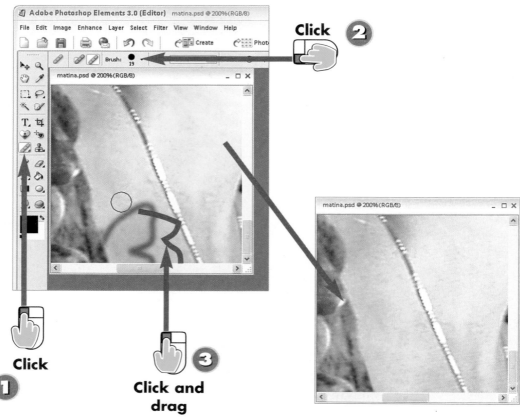

Click ②

Click ①

Click and drag ③

1. With a zoomed photo in the active image area, select the **Healing Brush** tool or press **J**.

2. Choose a brush size somewhat smaller than the area you want to fill in.

3. Click and drag across the area to paint it with texture copied from the surrounding area.

End

INTRODUCTION

Unlike the Spot Healing Brush, the Healing Brush tool requires you to paint back and forth across whatever you're trying to remove from the image. It's a better bet for fixing larger objects or areas that aren't completely surrounded by the same color or texture, such as tattoos, stray strands of hair, or distracting jewelry.

Odds Are It'll Be Even
You can use the Healing Brush to even out skin tones. Alt-click to place your source point in the area whose color you want to reproduce; select **Color** from the **Mode** drop-down menu on the **Options** bar.

Enhancing or Toning Down a Color

Start

Click
2

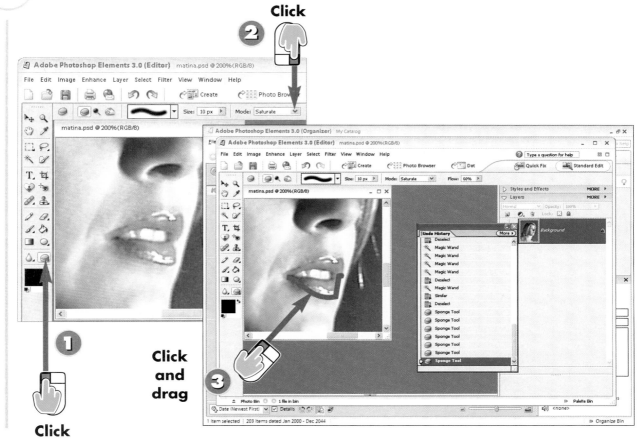

Click

①

**Click
and
drag**
3

Click

1. With a photo in the active image area, select the **Sponge** tool, or press **Q**.

2. To enhance color, select **Saturate** from the **Mode** drop-down menu in the options bar.

3. Click and drag over an area to heighten its color.

End

INTRODUCTION

The Sponge tool doesn't actually change the color of a selection, it just intensifies (saturates) or reduces (desaturates) it. It can come in handy for brightening up a wardrobe, such as neck scarves, or for toning down a too-colorful background that's competing with your subject.

TIP

Sponge Options
As with many other tools, the options bar offers a selection of brush tip sizes. The Flow setting controls the rate at which pixels become saturated or desaturated as you paint over them.

HINT

Dishwater Results?
If you overuse the Sponge in Desaturate mode, you'll remove all color from the area. That's fine if you're going for a selective monochrome look—or to make skin look downright ghostly.

Adding a Vignette to a Portrait

Start

Click

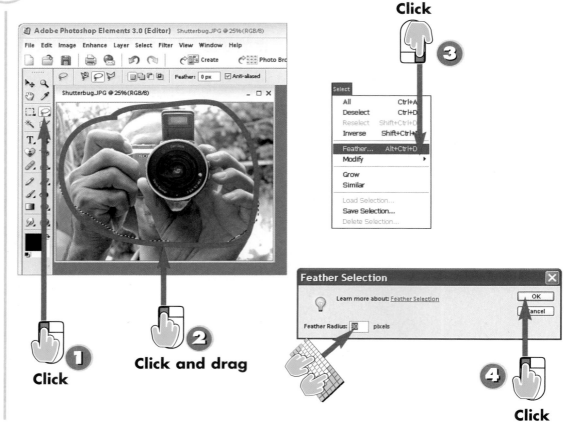

Click

Click and drag

Click

1. Select the **Lasso** tool.

2. Click and drag to trace around the subject of the portrait.

3. Choose **Select**, **Feather**, or press **Alt+Ctrl+D**.

4. Type a large **Feather Radius** (such as **30** pixels for a 5-inch 300 pixel/inch image). Click **OK**.

INTRODUCTION

Professional portraitists call a feathered photo a *vignette*, and it's been around ever since Matthew Brady aimed his camera at Civil War soldiers in the 1860s. Although you can use feathering to soften the edges of any selected area, its usual purpose is to convey sentimental feeling for the subject.

HINT

Noticeable Feather Radius

In step 4, the higher the resolution of the picture, the greater the Feather Radius should be. You might need to increase the setting to make the feathered edge large enough to be obvious.

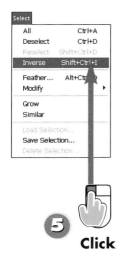

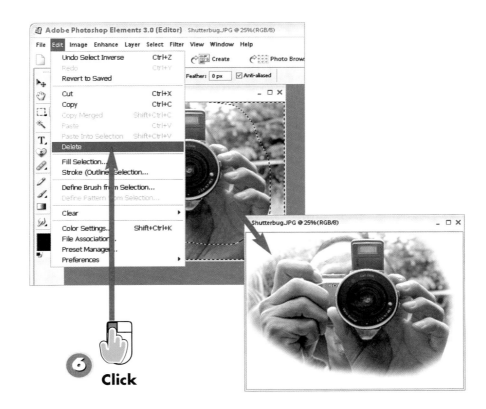

5 Click

6 Click

5 Choose **Select**, **Inverse**, or press **Shift+Ctrl+I**.

6 Choose **Edit**, **Delete**, or press **Del**.

 End

When to Use?
Vignette portraits can be particularly attractive when you frame them in oval or circular mattes and/or frames. And if you're going for an antique look, such as a sepia print, a vignette is the right finishing touch.

Selection Shape
Using the Rectangular Marquee or Elliptical Marquee tools gives more regular results than the Lasso and so might be a better choice if you're trying to fit your vignette image neatly inside a frame.

Adding a Soft Glow

1 With a portrait in the active image area, choose **Layer**, **Duplicate Layer**.

2 Click **OK**.

3 Choose **Filter**, **Blur**, **Gaussian Blur**.

4 Adjust the **Radius** of the blur for the amount of softening you want. Click **OK**.

Ever notice the glow around star-lets in black-and-white movies of the 20s and 30s? This *halation effect* was actually a flaw of early film, but audiences equated it with glamour. Soft focus is still a wonderful way to soften skin and hide pores.

Gaussian Blur Radius
The Gaussian Blur option controls the extent of blurring. The image changes as you adjust the slider. Make it blurred enough to lose unwanted detail, but sharp enough so the viewer can't immediately tell it's out of focus.

Preserving Layers
To preserve editable layers so you can return to the original image, save your work as a Photoshop (**.psd**) file. TIFF (**.tif**) files also have an option for saving layers.

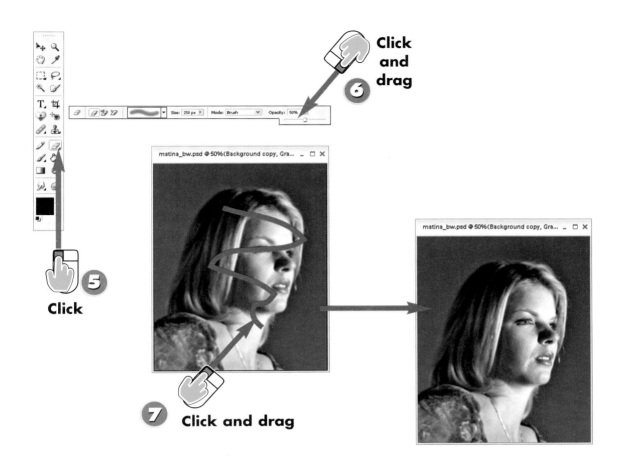

Click and drag

Click

Click
and
drag

5 Select the **Eraser** tool, or press **E**.

6 Adjust **Opacity** to **50%**.

7 Click and drag in the image to paint over and reveal facial details you want to remain sharp.

End

Clarify Important Details
If you sharpen facial features—such as eyes, nose, and mouth—viewers won't necessarily notice the rest is out of focus. Don't forget to sharpen important details, such as the necklace, in this case.

Do This Last
If you're doing a thorough retouching job on a portrait, use the other techniques described in this part first to reduce lines, and so on; then add the Gaussian blur last.

Trimming Contours on the Face or Body

Start

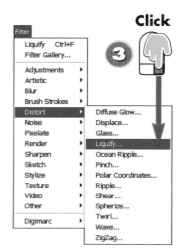

Click

1 Select the **Lasso** tool.

2 Click and drag around the contour to be reduced; make the inner edge of the selection along the line you want the contour to follow.

3 Select **Filter**, **Distort**, **Liquify**.

INTRODUCTION

We all have an unsightly bulge or two we wouldn't mind getting rid of, right? Well, forget diet and exercise—with the Liquify filter you can push that saggy skin right where you'd like it to be. No muss, no fuss!

Surgical Technique
The trick here is to choose an area that includes either side of an edge, such as a jaw or waistline, and then move it inward—toward the center of the face or body.

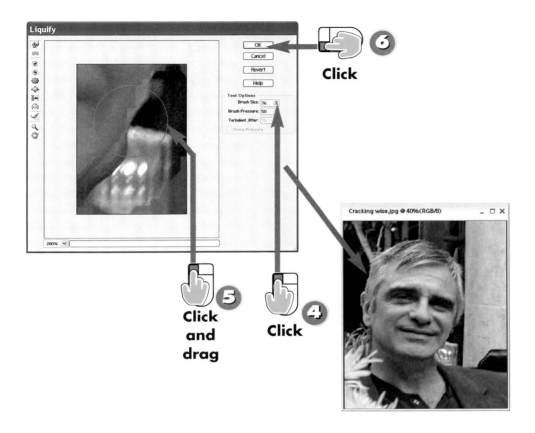

4 Select a brush one third to one half the size of the area you want to "tuck."

5 Click and drag toward the inner edge of the selection to reposition the skin.

6 Click **OK**.

End

Move By Itty Bits
Take it slow and easy when using the Liquify tool. The smaller your movements with the mouse, the more subtle the effect will be. Watch out for adjacent objects—try to drag so they won't be distorted.

Tidy Up
For a seamless transplant, you might need to use other retouching tools, such as Smudge or Clone Stamp, to clean up the edges.

Building Albums and Presentations

For some of us, it's all about getting published. It's all very well to learn how to retouch those family photos and jazz them up with cute drawings, but if you don't show them to anybody—what's the point?

Photoshop Elements has a feature called Web Photo Gallery that generates personal photo Web sites with very little effort. To publish your work to the Web, you need to get a Web hosting account. Many Internet service providers (ISPs) offer space for personal Web pages as part of their basic service, so if you have an account with an ISP, you might already have this available to you.

To venture further into the realm of multimedia and Internet publishing, you must load your finished digital images into some other applications. Microsoft PowerPoint for slideshows and Microsoft Word for printed documents (and Web pages) come to mind right away because so many people rely on them.

You can get a variety of even more impressive outputs from Photoshop Elements's Organizer mode, which enables you to publish catalogs of images on paper and onscreen, as well as 3D-Album, which makes dazzling screensavers and self-running shows.

Thanks for the Memories

Web Photo Gallery

Screensaver

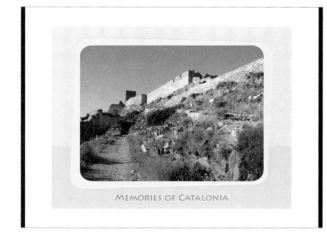

Greeting Card

Making a Web Photo Gallery

Start

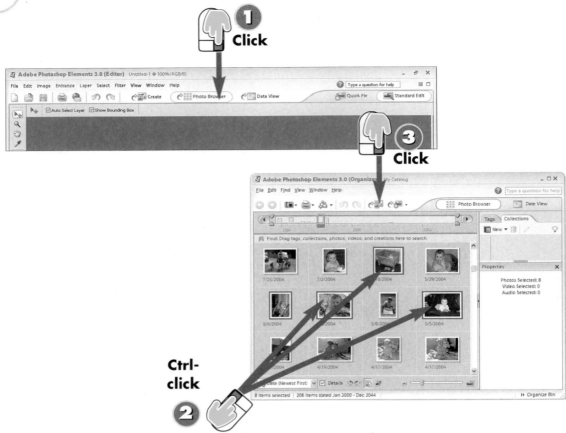

Click

Click

Ctrl-click

① Click **Photo Browser** to switch to Organizer mode.

② **Ctrl**-click to select the photos you want to include in your Web gallery.

③ Click **Create**.

Photoshop Elements includes a variety of designs for Web pages, and the program can automatically insert your photos and descriptive text into its templates with just a few clicks. It then generates completed pages ready for uploading to your Web hosting service or ISP.

HINT

Folder Your Photos
For quickest results, start by putting the photos you want to use in a separate folder. The order of the pictures on the pages will be alphabetical by filename.

TIP

Where Is It?
Elements saves the files for your Web gallery in the My Documents folder. If you want to save them in a different folder, click **Browse** in the Web Photo Gallery dialog box.

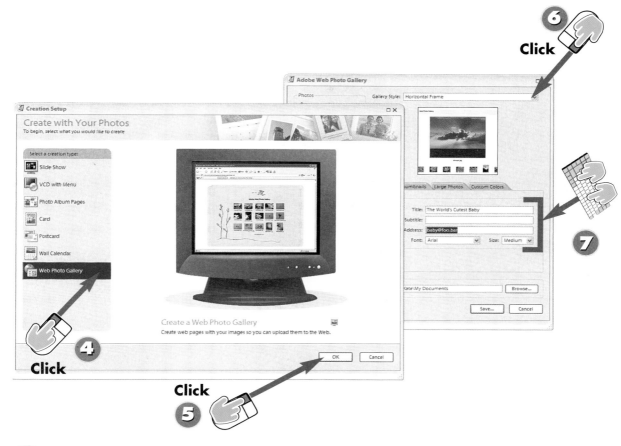

4 Click **Web Photo Gallery**.

5 Click **OK**.

6 Select an option from the **Gallery Style** drop-down menu, such as **Horizontal Frame**.

7 Enter a title for the gallery and (if you like) your email address to receive comments from viewers.

See next page

Want Mail?

TIP

Entering an email address in step 3 isn't mandatory, so just leave it blank if you don't want site visitors to contact you. If the E-mail text box is grayed, the style you selected can't display an address.

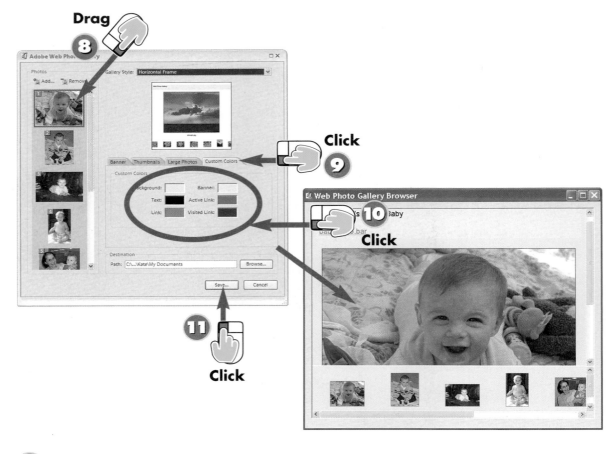

Drag

Click

Click

Click

8 Drag and drop the pictures in the **Photos** area to change their order.

9 Click the **Custom Colors** tab.

10 Click the color swatches to change the gallery's background and link colors.

11 Click **Save**.

End

INTRODUCTION

Follow instructions of your Web hosting service for uploading—*publishing*—your files. The usual method is via the *File Transfer Protocol (FTP)*. A handy and inexpensive program for doing this is GlobalSCAPE CuteFTP.

TIP

What Is That Again?
To include captions, select either **Filename** or **Caption** in the Captions area of the Thumbnails tab; then choose a font and size. To store caption information, see "Adding and Printing Photo Captions" on p. 74.

TIP

Where's That Picture?
If you realize in the midst of setting options for your Web gallery that you've left out your favorite photo, click **Add** in the **Photos** section to return to the Organizer and select it.

Loading Your Photos into the Organizer

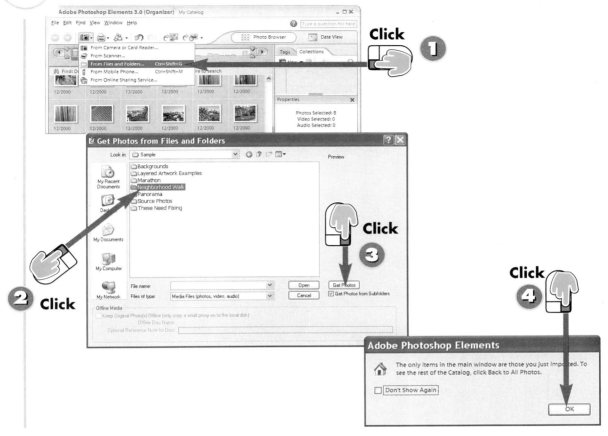

1 From the Organizer's Get Photos drop-down menu, choose **From Files and Folders**, or press **Ctrl+Shift+G**.

2 Navigate to the folder that contains your pictures, and click its thumbnail (or file-name).

3 Click the **Get Photos** button.

4 Click **OK**. The photos in the selected folder are loaded into a new catalog. You can now create an album or presentation.

End

With Element's Photoshop Organizer, you can create albums, slideshows, greeting cards, Web galleries, video CDs, e-cards, calendars, photo books, and 3D galleries. But to do any of this, you must first load your pictures into the application to create a *catalog*.

Get Organized
Photoshop Elements also provides ways of organizing your growing photo collection. But the easiest way to create an album or show is to put all the photos in a folder on your hard drive (or other media) first, as suggested here.

Building an Album in the Organizer

Start

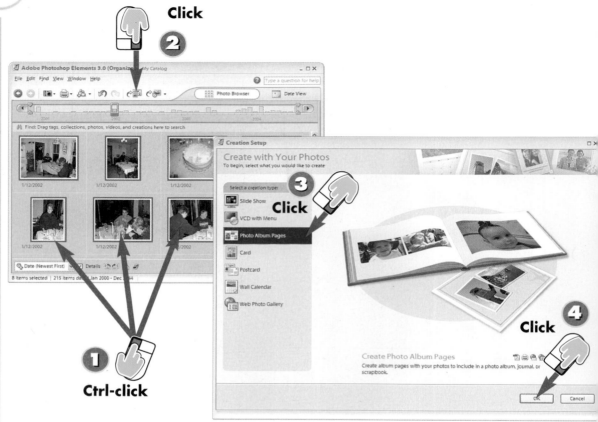

Click

Ctrl-click

Click

Click

1. In the Organizer, select the photos you want to include in your printed album pages.

2. Click the **Create** button.

3. Click **Photo Album Pages**.

4. Click **OK**.

A traditional-style printed photo album is just one of the creations available. The other selections that have much the same steps as Photo Album Pages are Slide Show, VCD with Menu, Card, Postcard, and Wall Calendar.

What's a VCD?
VCD stands for Video CD—it's a CD format you can write with your computer's CD-R or CD-RW drive and play in most DVD players. VCDs work much like DVDs, but they can hold only a tenth of the data.

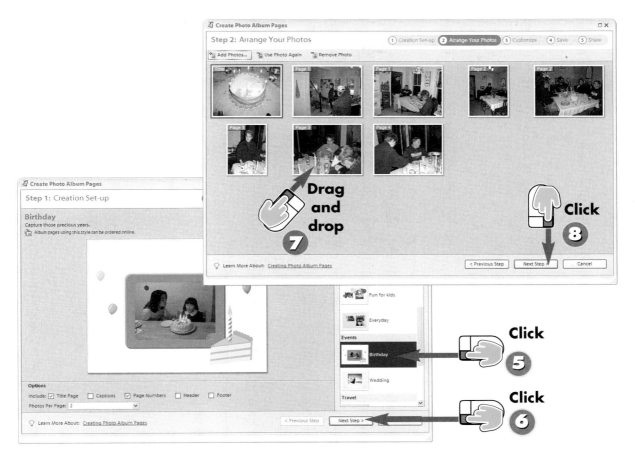

⑤ Select an album style, such as **Birthday**.

⑥ Click **Next Step**.

⑦ Drag and drop the photos into the order you want for the album pages.

⑧ Click **Next Step**.

See next page

HINT

A 1000-Word Picture
The first photo in your grouping appears on your album's title page, so make sure it's one that reflects the spirit of the event, people, or places you're documenting in these album pages.

TIP

Selecting Photos
If you start by importing all the photos you need from a folder, you don't need to go looking for them in step 1. Regardless, you have the option to add photos, duplicate photos, or delete photos from the catalog in step 7 by using the buttons located just above the images.

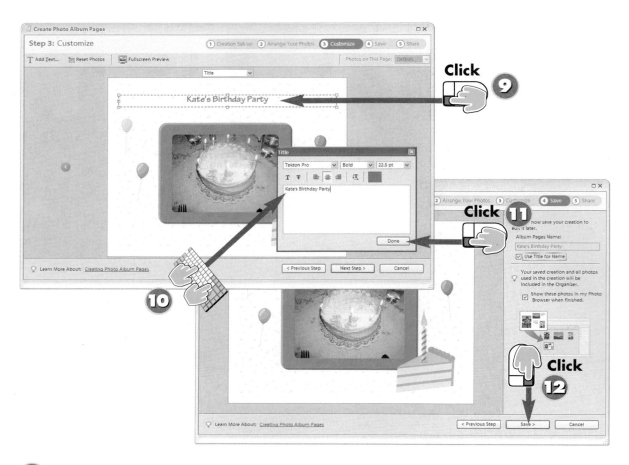

9 Click the album title placeholder to add your own title.

10 Type in the new album title.

11 Click **Done**.

12 Click **Save**.

End

Output Options

After you click Save in step 12, you have the options of printing your pages, saving them in Adobe Reader (PDF) format, sending the album as an email attachment, burning a CD, or ordering professional photo prints online.

Creating a PowerPoint Photo Slideshow

Start

Click **1**

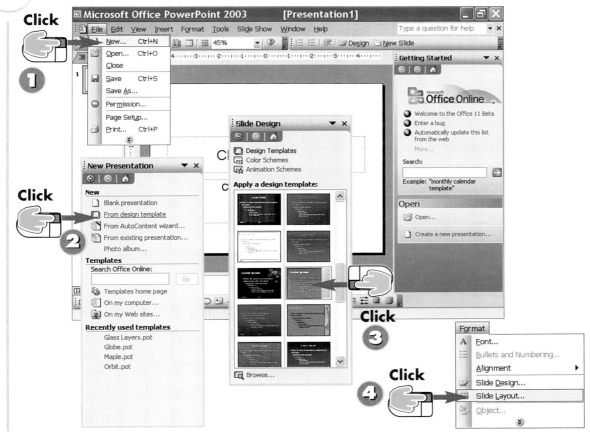

Click **2**

Click **3**

Click **4**

1 In Microsoft PowerPoint, choose **File**, **New**, or press **Ctrl+N**.

2 In the New Presentation task pane, select **From Design Template**.

3 Click a design template in a style you like.

4 Choose **Format**, **Slide Layout**.

See next page

INTRODUCTION

Photoshop Elements can create electronic slideshows all by itself. But many folks already have PowerPoint (part of the Office suite), so here's how to make a series of photo slides with titles in just a few steps.

HINT

PowerPoint's Graphics
PowerPoint has its own graphics tools for adding text and drawings to your slides. If you want to modify the image itself, use Photoshop Elements. For objects that surround it on the slide, use the PowerPoint tools.

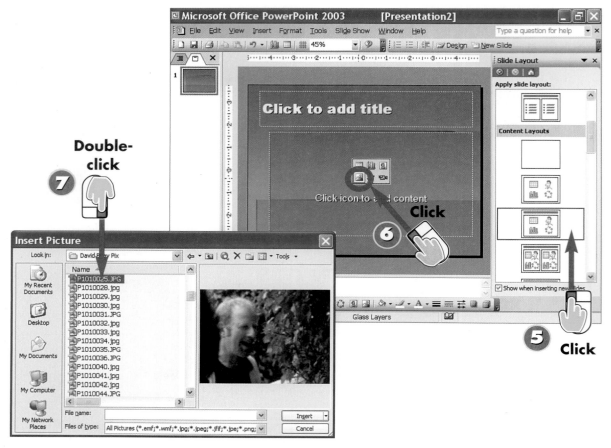

5 Click a Content Layout in the Slide Layout task pane, such as **Title with Content**.

6 In the slide area, click **Insert Picture**.

7 Navigate to the folder that contains the picture, and double-click its filename. The picture is inserted into the slide.

Insert in Any Slide
Any of the content layouts are best for making slides that contain photos, but you can add a picture from an external file to any slide by choosing **Insert**, **Picture**, **From File**.

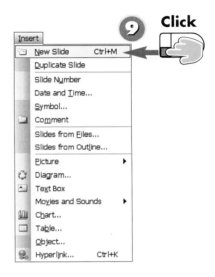

8 Select the default title text field and then type a title for the slide.

9 Choose **Insert**, **New Slide**, or press **Ctrl+M**. (Repeat these steps for every slide in the presentation; then save your work.)

End

INTRODUCTION
This task was done using PowerPoint 2003. Even though their screens look different, earlier versions of PowerPoint (97 and 2000) work much the same way. As an alternative, Photoshop Album 2 can also generate slideshows.

TIP
Running Your Show
After you're finished, save your work. Then choose **View**, **Slide Show** (or press F5) to display the show on your computer screen. Press the **spacebar** or **PageDown** to advance to the next slide. Press **Esc** to exit the show.

HINT
Emailing Your Show
To create a show that's viewable on most PCs that don't have the PowerPoint software on them, choose **File**, **Save As** and select the **PowerPoint Show (.pps)** file type.

Creating a Screensaver Show with 3D-Album

Start

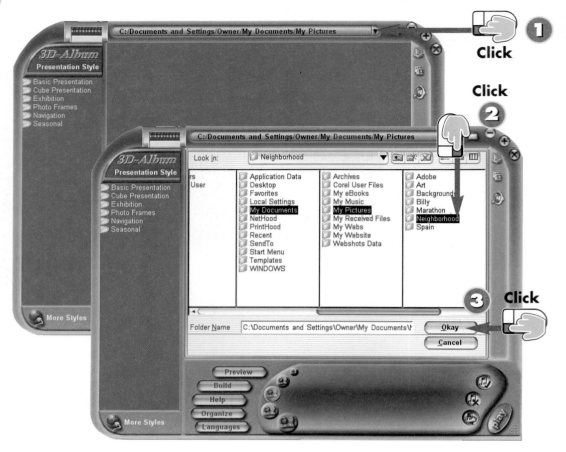

1. In 3D-Album, click the **Album Folder** drop-down menu.

2. Select the folder that contains the photos you want to use.

3. Click **Okay**.

INTRODUCTION

Micro Research Institute 3D-Album™ can generate self-running slideshows, screensavers, Web pages, and email attachments. You'll find a version of 3D-Album on the companion CD. Its animated screensavers are particularly cool.

Adobe's 3D Shows

HINT

Photoshop Elements's output options include Atmosphere 3D Gallery, which generates an animated *virtual walkthrough*, a tour of imaginary rooms as a series of Web pages. But it doesn't make screensavers or self-running shows.

4 Select a Presentation Style, such as **Exhibition**, **Exhibit Island**. Click **Build**.

5 Select **Create Presentation As a Screensaver**.

6 Type an identifying name for the screensaver selection.

7 Click **Build**.

End

Finishing Up
After the screensaver has been built, you see a message dialog box. Click **Okay** and close 3D-Album. Your new screensaver is now the current setting for the Windows Desktop.

Screensaver Settings
To change your screensaver, right-click an empty space on the Windows Desktop, select **Properties**, click the **Screen Saver** tab, make a new selection in the **Screen Saver** drop-down menu, and click **OK**.

Using Layers to Combine Photos and Artwork

If you know how animated movies were made in the days before computer generation, you're already familiar with the concept of layers. Animation artists traditionally used a process called *ink-and-paint* to draw cartoon characters on transparent sheets of celluloid, or *cels*. One new cel had to be created for each time a character moved. Cels were then placed over elaborate painted backgrounds, such as witches' castles or the decks of pirate ships. Painting on separate layers—the animated character on the cel and the background beneath—made it possible to reuse the same background throughout a long scene.

Layers in Photoshop Elements work much the same way. The image you begin with is the Background layer. Every layer you add starts out as transparent until you change its color, change its adjustment properties, or add objects to it.

If you've done any of the tasks in other parts involving shapes or text, you were working with layers, whether you realized it or not. Understand, building more complex layered images isn't for beginners. But you should learn some of this if you want to graduate to more ambitious tasks.

The postcard on the facing page is actually built from 10 layers, including the background. Photoshop Elements permits you as many as 8,000 layers—provided you don't run out of computer memory first!

A Ten-Layered Image

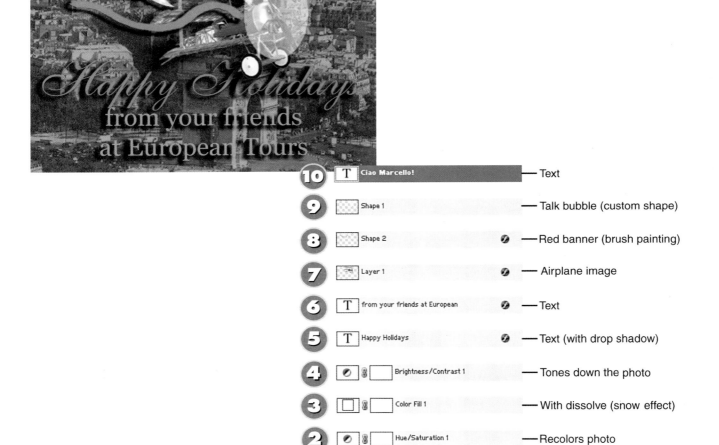

Painting on a New Layer

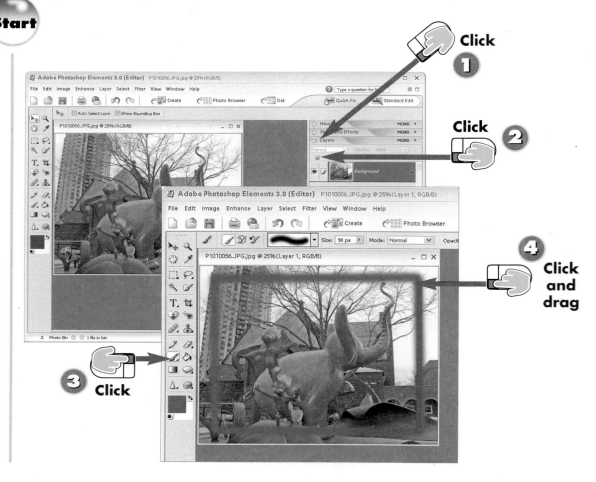

Start

Click ①

Click ②

Click ③

Click and drag ④

---

① Open or undock the **Layers** palette (or choose **Window**, **Layers**).

② Click the **Create a New Layer** button (or choose **Layer**, **New**, **Layer**).

③ Select a tool, such as **Brush**.

④ Paint on the layer.

End

TIP

Simplify and Merge

Simplifying changes vector shapes and text (based on geometry) to pixels—editable as dots, not as shapes. Merging both simplifies the active (selected) layer and combines it with the layer beneath.

You can't manipulate text and shapes as objects after merging. If you see a warning that the layer must be simplified before proceeding with a tool, choose **Cancel** and create a new layer using these steps; then reselect the tool and paint or draw.

Copying an Object to a New Layer

Start

Click

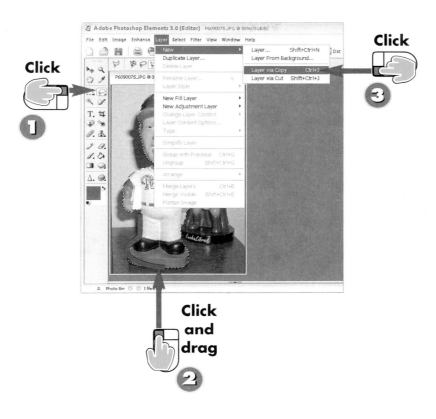

Click

3

1

**Click
and
drag**

2

1. Click a selection tool, such as **Lasso**.

2. Select the object to be copied to a new layer.

3. Choose **Layer**, **New**, **Layer via Copy**.

End

INTRODUCTION

Selecting an object on the background layer, making changes, and then saving your work, changes the original image forever. Instead, use these steps to copy a selected object to a new layer, leaving the background layer unchanged.

TIP

Cutting a Selection
The command **Layer**, **New**, **Layer via Cut** works just the same way, but it also deletes the selection from the original layer. Especially if the original layer is the Background, use **Layer via Copy** instead.

TIP

Deleting or Hiding
As long as the original layer is intact, you can always hide or delete the copied layer (**Layer**, **Delete Layer**) to cancel all its changes with a click.

Repositioning a Layer

Start

Click
2

Click
1

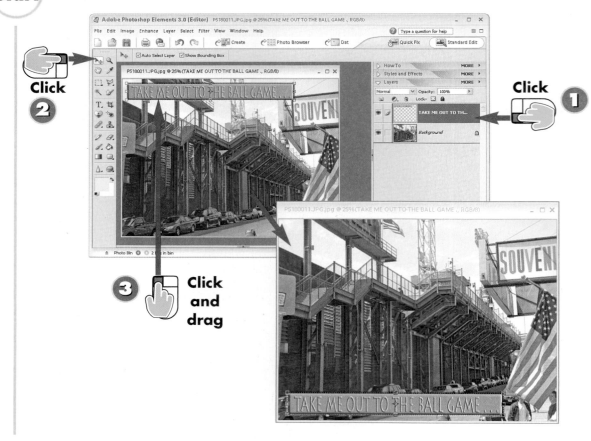

3 **Click and drag**

End

1 Select the name of the layer in the Layers palette.

2 Select the **Move** tool.

3 Click and drag the layer to reposition it in relation to the image area (or nudge it with the arrow keys, or **Shift-click** to constrain it as you drag).

INTRODUCTION

When you moved text and shapes in previous tasks, you might not have realized you were actually repositioning an entire layer, including not only the selection but also the transparent pixels surrounding it. In this image, the plane and the sky are on separate layers, and the task moves the entire layer higher in the sky.

HINT

Auto Select Layer
If Auto Select Layer is checked in the Move tool's options bar, the layer selection (the active layer) changes automatically when you click an object that resides on it. Remember that doing so actually moves the entire layer, not just the object.

TIP

More Button
Clicking **More** in the top-right corner of the Layers palette brings up a menu of commands that affect layers (handy alternative to the Layers menu).

Controlling Layers

Start

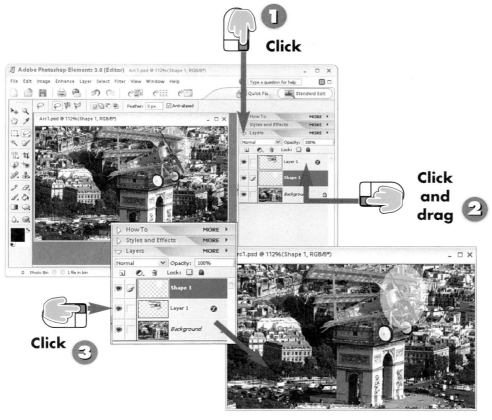

1 Click

2 Click and drag

3 Click

1 Open or undock the Layers palette (or choose **Window**, **Layers**).

2 To change the order of layers, click and drag the layer name to a new position, higher or lower on the list.

3 To hide any layer, causing it not to display or print, click the **Eye** icon. (To restore its visibility, click the Eye icon again.)

End

INTRODUCTION
The icons in the columns to the left of the layers in the palette control various layer behaviors such as locking a layer (preventing changes), creating and deleting a layer, hiding/unhiding a layer, new fill/adjustment layers, and *linking* layers.

TIP
Linking Layers
Link any layer to the active one by clicking the column to the left of the layer name in the Layers palette. A Link icon appears there. Some commands and operations, such as the Move tool, affect all linked layers at once.

TIP
Grouping Layers
The purpose of grouping layers is to control visibility of their objects according to a *base* layer. To group a layer with the one below, choose **Layer**, **Group with Previous**.

Creating a Fill Layer and Adjusting Layer Opacity

Start

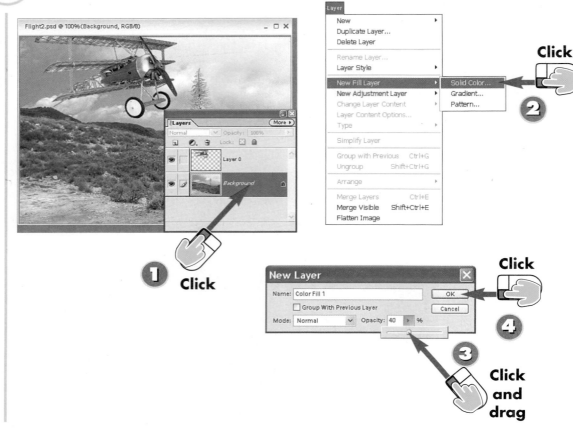

Click

②

① **Click**

Click

③

④

Click and drag

① Select the layer in the Layers palette above which the new layer will be inserted.

② Choose **Layer**, **New Fill Layer**, **Solid Color**.

③ Click and drag the **Opacity** slider to change how transparent the new layer is.

④ Click **OK**.

One way to change how layers look is to adjust the *opacity* of a fill layer above them. Think of a *semitransparent* fill layer (less than 100 percent opacity) as a colored photographic filter—tinting and dimming the layers beneath it. (The more opaque, the less transparent, and vice versa.)

HINT

To Bin or Not to Bin
Drag a palette out of the Palette Bin if you want to move it around on the screen. That way you can put it right next to the area of the image you're working on, or you can close the Palette bin to enlarge your work area but still use the palette.

HINT

Well Adjusted
Continuing to add other adjustment and fill layers, each with its own properties, will have a combined effect. Remember that an adjustment layer only affects the appearance of the layers *beneath* it; all affect the background.

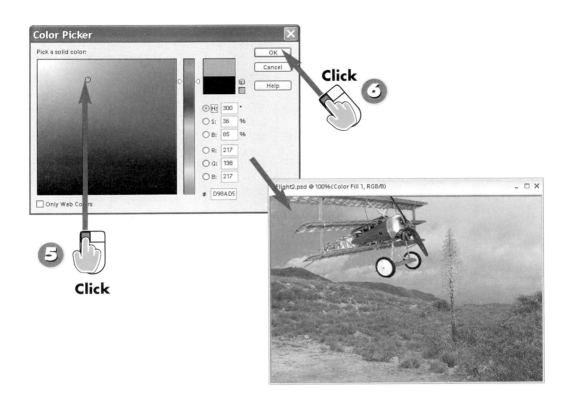

5. Click to select a fill color.

6. Click **OK**.

End

Special Effects

By using either the Gradient or Pattern submenu commands instead of Solid Color, you can create variegated effects: Gradient could cause the filtration effect to fade across the background; Pattern could give it a texture, like a dust storm.

Gradient and Pattern Fills

Besides Solid Color, other submenu selections available in step 2 are Gradient and Pattern, which have the same options as the Gradient tool and the Pattern settings of the Paint Bucket tool.

Flipping or Rotating a Layer

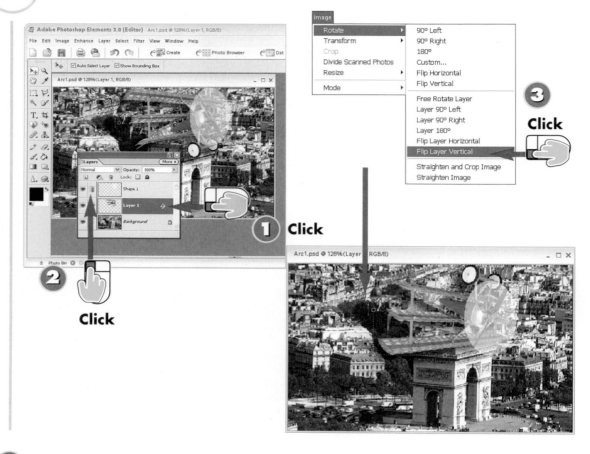

Start

1 Click

2 Click

3 Click

Click

1 Select the layer name in the Layers palette to make it the *active*, or current, layer.

2 Click the **Link** icon in the Layers palette to link any other layers that must be included in the operation.

3 Choose **Image**, **Rotate** and choose from the second group of submenu commands such as Flip Layer Vertical.

End

INTRODUCTION

The purpose of flipping or rotating a layer can be either to change the position of the objects on the layer or to vary the effect of a gradient or pattern layer. The Image, Rotate command has a submenu section for such operations performed on entire layers.

TIP

Selections or Layers?
When part of the image within a layer—such as a shape or text—is selected, the second group of commands in the Image, Rotate submenu switch from Layer to Selection. They have the same effect but only on the selected area.

Using an Adjustment Layer

Start

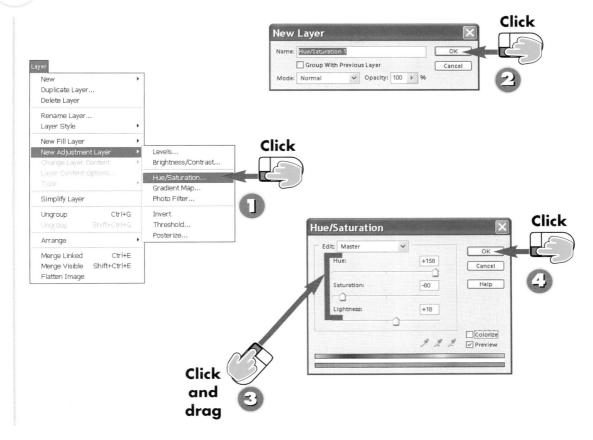

Click

Click

Click

Click and drag

1. Having selected the layer you want to control, choose **Layer**, **New Adjustment Layer** and select from the submenu commands, such as **Hue/Saturation**.

2. Click **OK**.

3. Make adjustments using the options in the dialog box and see the effect on your image in the background.

4. When you are satisfied with the effect, click **OK**.

End

INTRODUCTION

An adjustment layer has no color of its own but lets you control color, brightness/contrast, and other factors on layers beneath without making changes directly to them. The adjustment layer has no effect on layers above it unless you link or group them to the layer or layers below it.

TIP

Select a Layer First
The new adjustment layer will be inserted just above the layer that's active when you begin step 1. So if you want to adjust the background image, select that layer first and then do these steps.

HINT

Blending Mode
As described in the next task, the effect of any fill or adjustment layer can also be controlled by selecting a Blending Mode from the More menu in the Layers palette (or Mode menu in the New Layer dialog box).

Using Blending Modes on Layers

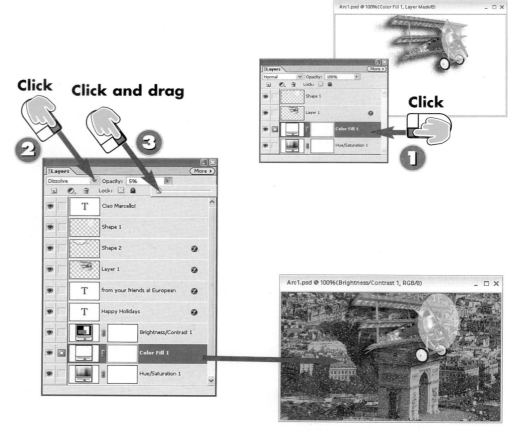

1. Select the layer name in the Layers palette to make it the active layer.

2. Select a blending mode, such as **Dissolve**.

3. Adjust the **Opacity** setting to control the extent of blending.

INTRODUCTION

Blending mode controls how pixel values within a layer are blended with those of the layers beneath. The default is Normal. Other modes include Dissolve, several Dodge or Burn effects, quality of light (such as Soft or Hard), adding (Exclusion) or subtracting (Difference) pixel values, or individual elements of color.

TIP

Try 'Em On
After making a selection from the blending mode list in step 2, press the **Up** or **Down** arrow keys to step through the other modes and preview their effects on the image.

TIP

Controlling Blending Mode
To turn off a blending mode, change the setting back to **Normal** for that layer in the drop-down box in the top-left corner of the Layers palette.

Copying and Pasting a Layer Style

Start

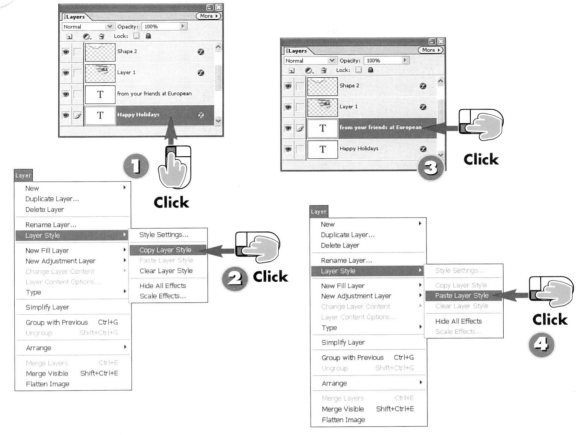

Click

Click

Click

Click

1. Select the name in the Layers palette of a layer that contains a layer style, such as **Drop Shadow**.

2. Choose **Layer**, **Layer Style**, **Copy Layer Style**.

3. Select the name of a layer to which the style will be applied.

4. Choose **Layer**, **Layer Style**, **Paste Layer Style**.

End

INTRODUCTION

Copying layer styles is particularly convenient when you've made several style changes on one layer and want to apply them with a click to all objects on another layer—also if you've taken pains to fine-tune a style, such as adjusted the angle of a drop-shadow.

TIP

Fine-Tuning Styles
To fine-tune a layer style on the active layer, such as Bevel or Drop Shadow, choose **Layer**, **Layer Style**, **Style Settings**. Make adjustments by clicking and dragging the sliders; and then click **OK**.

Preparing to Publish

With Photoshop Elements, a digital camera, a computer, and an inexpensive color inkjet printer, you can be your own one-stop shop for most of your photography needs. But there's a whole wide world out there—including a giant color printing industry—ready to serve you.

Need custom-printed tee shirts? Color posters? Banners? A thousand color postcards? These days, most commercial printers accept—and actually prefer—your Photoshop image files as source artwork for these kinds of printing jobs. You can even submit your orders online at sites such as **www.vistaprint.com**, **www.inkchaser.com**, and **www.kinkos.com**.

Admittedly, preparing files for commercial printing is a major reason why some serious graphic artists consider upgrading to "big Photoshop" (Adobe Photoshop CS). Specifically, that application has extensive *color management* capabilities that Photoshop Elements lacks.

But there's still a lot you can do in Photoshop Elements to improve the quality of the results when you decide to "send it out"—whether you're publishing on paper or via electronic media.

How Do I Get from Here to There?

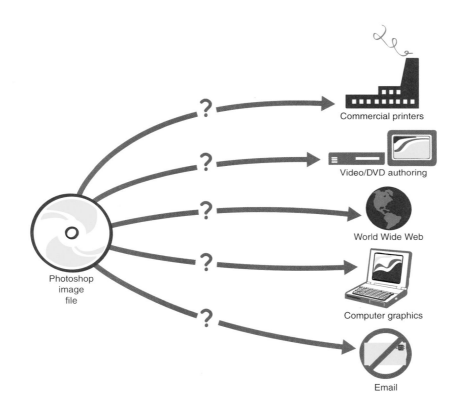

Commercial printers

Video/DVD authoring

World Wide Web

Computer graphics

Photoshop image file

Email

Fixing Multiple Images

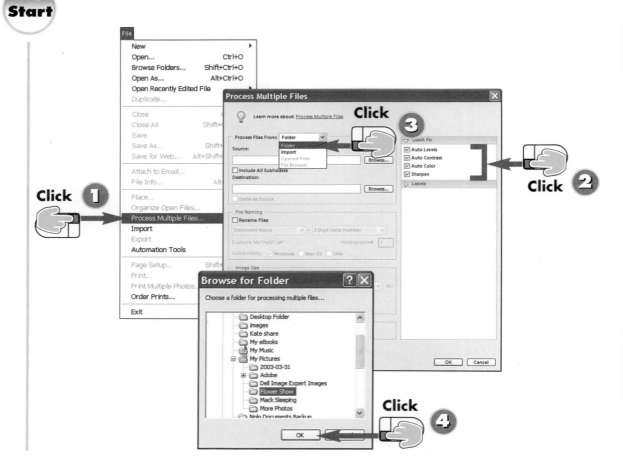

1. Select **File**, **Process Multiple Files**.

2. Select the **Quick Fix** operations you want to apply.

3. Select **Folder** from the **Process Files from** drop-down menu.

4. Navigate to the folder of images you want to process; then click **OK**.

Have a bunch of pictures that need fixing? You can have Photoshop Elements do the work while you refill your coffee cup. Enjoy a break while Elements adjusts the lighting, color, and sharpness of your images; resizes them; renames them; and saves them in your preferred format.

TIP

Get Organized First
Be sure to put all the image files you want to process in a single folder, so Elements will be able to find them. The program can process only a single folder at a time—although it can process all the folders within a folder.

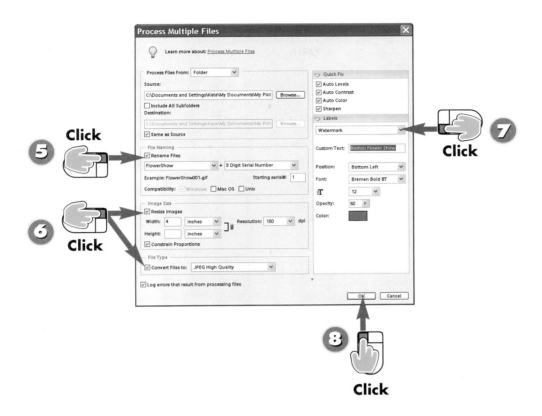

Click **5**

Click **6**

Click **7**

Click

Click **8**

5 Select **Rename Files** to automatically give the files consistent names.

6 Select **Resize Images** and **Convert Files to** to resize the images and save them in a different format.

7 Select **Watermark** to add overlaid labels to the images.

8 Click **OK** to begin processing.

End

What's a Watermark?
A *watermark* is a semitranspar-ent design or line of text over-laid on an image to identify it. It's a great way to ensure everyone knows your pictures are yours without obscuring their details.

Be Careful
Don't select Same as Source under Destination unless you don't want to keep your origi-nal files. With this option turned on, Elements overwrites the originals with the revised ver-sions.

Previewing a Halftone Image for Color Printing

Start

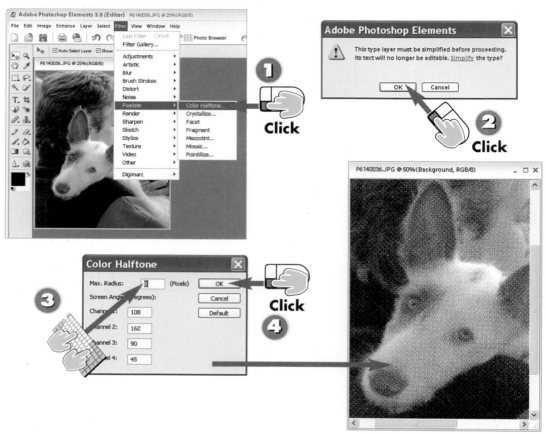

1. With a color picture in the active image area, choose **Filter**, **Pixelate**, **Color Halftone**.

2. If a simplify warning appears, click **OK**.

3. Type a number between **4** and **127** for **Max. Radius** to control the size of the halftone dots.

4. Click **OK**.

End

INTRODUCTION

Halftone screens break images into collections of tiny dots for conventional printing. Photoshop Elements lacks the features to convert imagery to true halftones but can show you how images would look if reproduced by this method. The printing service to which you submit your files can convert them.

HINT

Resolution and Radius
The lower the resolution of your image, the lower the Max Radius setting must be. A setting of 4 is about right for a 300 dpi image.

HINT

Don't Sweat the Angles
Don't mess with the Screen Angles settings unless your printer tells you to vary them.

Previewing a Halftone Image for B&W Printing

Start

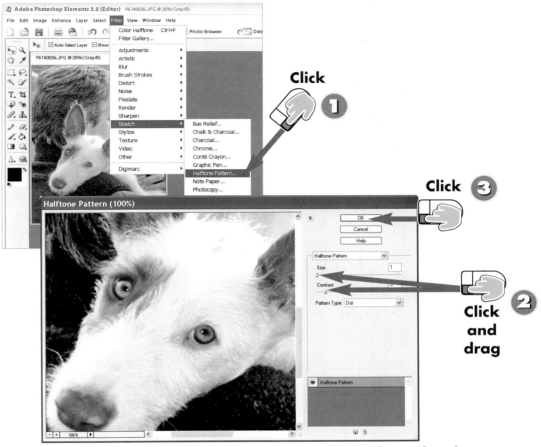

Click ①

Click ③

Click and drag ②

① With a grayscale picture in the active image area, choose **Filter**, **Sketch**, **Halftone Pattern**.

② Adjust the sliders to control dot **Size** and **Contrast**.

③ Click **OK**.

End

INTRODUCTION
As with color halftones, this Sketch filter is simply a way of previewing how a grayscale image would look in print. Some designers also use it as an artistic effect. The main thing to remember about a halftone image is that, although it appears to have grayscale shading, every dot in the image is pure black.

HINT
Other Pattern Types
Most conventional printing processes use the Dot pattern. Alternatives are Circle and Line.

Using Color Management for Commercial Printing

Start

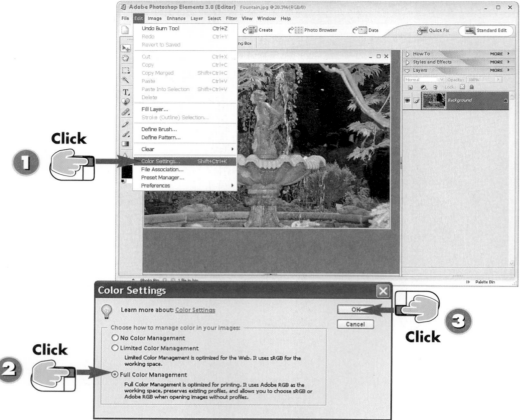

Click ①

Click ②

Click ③

① With a picture in the active image area, choose **Edit**, **Color Settings** or press **Shift+Ctrl+K**.

② Click **Full Color Management**.

③ Click **OK**.

An important part of submitting your digital files for color printing is to be able to match color accurately. Apply color management to any file you send out to a commercial printer. To adjust CMYK color and to generate Prepress PDF files, you'll have to upgrade to Photoshop CS.

TIP

Paper or Screen?
In step 2, select **Limited Color Management** if you will be publishing on the Web instead of in print.

Click

Click

Click

4 Choose **File**, **Save As**, or press **Shift+Ctrl+S**.

5 Check the **ICC Profile** box.

6 Click **Save**.

End

What's Your Profile?

Profiles are standardized color tables used by the printing industry. Adobe has been an industry leader in making it possible to match digital outputs with conventional printing methods.

Why Bother?

Important reasons to worry about *color matching* are when you are trying to reproduce product photography (particularly food, which must look realistic and appetizing) and company logos, which have precise color requirements.

Preparing a Still Image for Video

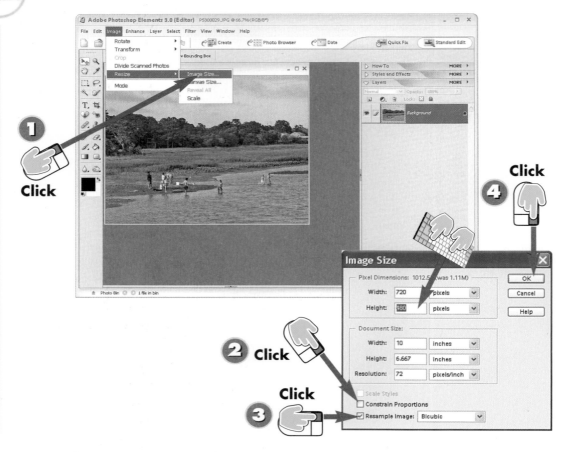

Start

Click ①

Click ②

Click ③

Click ④

① Start with an image that's 720×540 pixels open in the active image area. Choose **Image**, **Resize**, **Image Size**.

② Uncheck **Constrain Proportions**.

③ Check **Resample Image**.

④ Keeping the Width at 720, change **Height** to **480** pixels and click **OK**.

A curious problem arises from the fact that computer images have square pixels, but in digital video they're rectangular. You might think this an odd technicality, but if you make video titles or DVD menus in Photoshop Elements and don't follow these steps, the images will look squished when you convert them to video.

What's Your System?
Digital video (DV) editing is coming to a PC near you. Windows Movie Maker, Apple iMovie, and Pinnacle Studio are examples of the many applications available for assembling your home movie footage in creative ways.

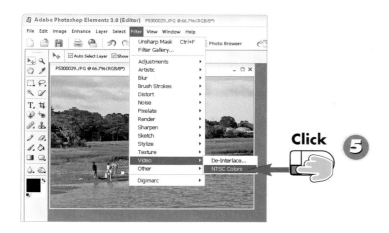

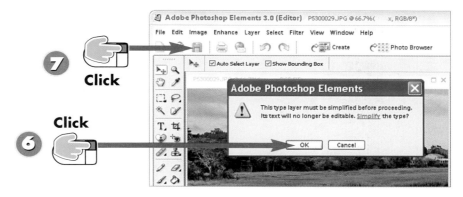

5 Choose **Filter**, **Video**, **NTSC Colors**.

6 If you see a simplify warning, click **OK**.

7 Click **Save**.

End

DVD Menus
One challenge of creating a DVD is to build the menu system by which users can make program selections. Many DVD authoring programs can use still imagery you create as Photoshop files for menus.

NTSC Color
This color model applies to broadcast television in North America. You'll need a different plug-in for the UK or France/Asia.

Sending a Picture via Email

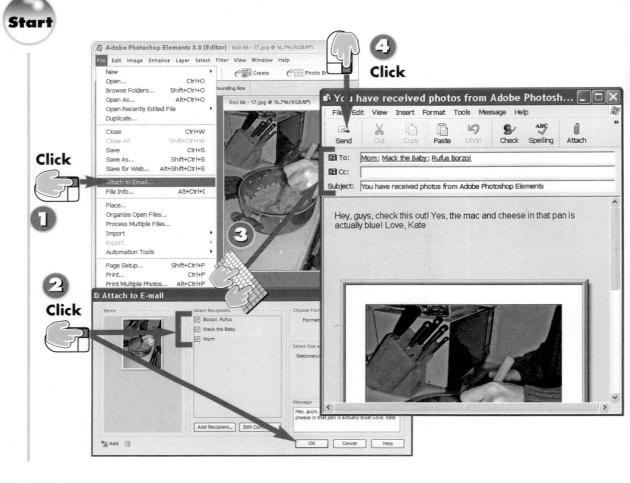

1 With a JPEG picture in the active image area, choose **File**, **Attach to Email**.

2 Choose recipients for the email and click **OK**.

3 Type the recipient's email address in the **To** field. (Or click **To:** to select from your Address Book.) Also type a **Subject** and **Message**.

4 Click **Send**.

End

The secret to sending pictures via email is to make the files compact without sacrificing too much quality. Even though any file converted for the Web will also do nicely for email, Photoshop Elements has this handy built-in feature that both automatically resizes the photo and attaches it to an outgoing email message.

Sender Beware!
TIP

Certain types of computer viruses can hide out in image files, so install virus protection such as Norton Antivirus or McAfee VirusScan and set it to check all outgoing email attachments automatically.

Converting to Indexed Color for the Web

Start

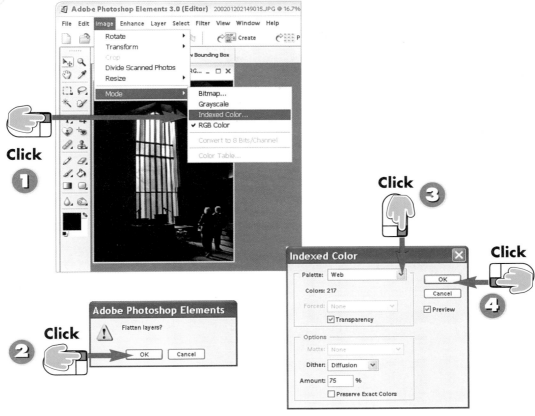

Click 1

Click 3

Click 4

Click 2

Adobe Photoshop Elements

Flatten layers?

OK   Cancel

---

1 Choose **Image**, **Mode**, **Indexed Color**.

2 If this warning appears, click **OK** to flatten all layers.

3 Set Palette to **Web**.

4 Click **OK**.

End

INTRODUCTION
Desktop computers of various vintages differ in the number of video colors they can show. To ensure that Web imagery can be viewed on most of them, Photoshop Elements has this feature for converting and restricting an image to the 256 colors most computers can display.

HINT
Palette Types
As long as you are creating for the Web (the main reason for using indexed color), the other palette types needn't concern you. If you're making graphics for use in a Windows program, select **System**.

TIP
Index Color Options
Selecting the **Diffusion** option for Dithering should make the best Web pictures. *Dithering* groups dots of two or more indexed colors together to simulate subtler colors.

Optimizing a Picture for the Web

Start

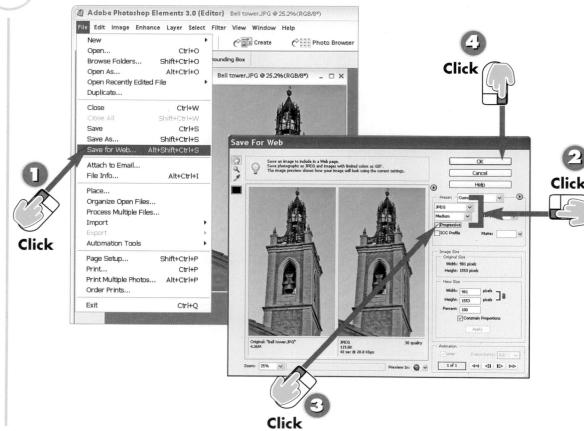

Click

Click

Click

Click

1. With your finished picture in the active image area, choose **File**, **Save for Web**.

2. In the Presets box, select a picture format and quality, such as **JPEG Medium**.

3. Optionally, check the **Progressive** box.

4. Click **OK**.

INTRODUCTION

Preparing an image for the Web involves converting its file type to JPEG, GIF, or PNG; restricting its colors to 256; reducing its size to a few inches wide; and limiting its resolution to 72 pixels/inch.

Control File Size
You can use the Image, Resize, Image Size command to size the image to the computer screen (typically, 2–4 inches wide), with resolution of 72 pixels/inch.

5 Click

5 Click **Save**.

End

Progressive Mode
Selecting **Progressive** mode for a JPEG file causes it to be displayed in stages as it downloads, resulting in a more pleasing experience for users with relatively slow (dial-up) connections.

Control Image Size
To capture the interest of Web surfers, you want your home page to load as quickly as possible. Keep images there to thumbnail size; then permit interested viewers to click on them to download higher-resolution pictures.

Saving As an Animated Picture for the Web

Start

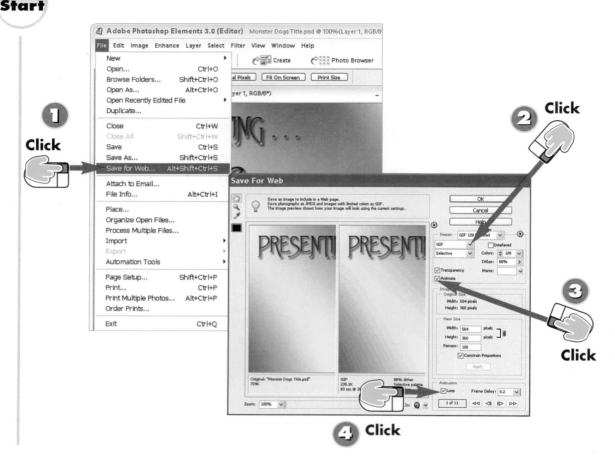

Click

Click 2

3 **Click**

4 **Click**

1 With a multilayered image in the active image area, choose **File**, **Save for Web**.

2 In the Presets section, select **GIF** as the picture type.

3 Check the **Animate** box.

4 In the Animation section, check the **Loop** box (for continuous playback).

These conversion steps take any layered file and convert it to a series of GIF frames (animated .gif file). Displayed on a Web page in rapid succession, a simple but effective animation sequence can be created. For example, text on successive layers appears to pop onto a background image.

Easy Animation

TIP

You can control the animated sequence by reordering the layers of your image in the Layers palette before you convert to GIF.

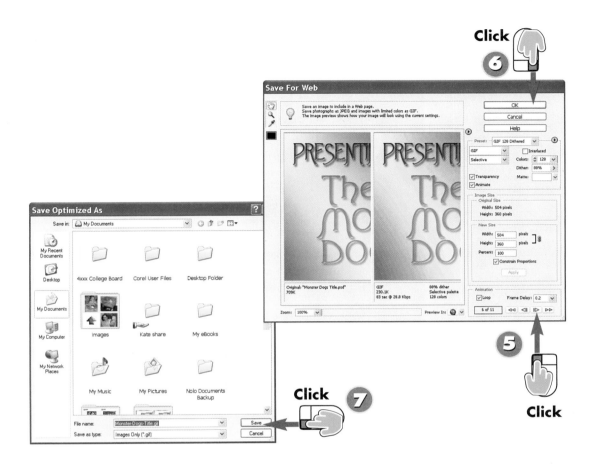

5 Step through to preview the animation by clicking the **Next Frame** button.

6 Click **OK**.

7 Click **Save**.

End

Frame Delay
This option in the Animation section of the Save for Web window lets you vary the delay between frames (layers) from 0 to 10 seconds. If you don't check Loop, the sequence plays once and stops.

Layered Imagery
Native Photoshop (**.psd**) files make excellent source material for this type of animation. For example, text can appear to pop onto a background. Creating different text layers can cause a message to be built up in steps.

Choosing Output File Types

As long as you're working for Me-Myself-and-I Productions—taking pictures, manipulating them, and printing them—stick with the Adobe Photoshop format, and you'll live happily ever after.

But the minute you want to share your stuff with the rest of the world, you face a bundle of challenges. For example, as some of the tasks in Part 10 show, if you want to post your pictures on the Web or send them via email, you need to convert the files to a *compressed* format such as JPEG.

For other purposes, such as creating artwork for publication, the choices can make your head swim. In those situations, tasks in this part can help you cut through the techno-babble and pick the right horse to run the course.

Many of these choices have to do with file *compression*. Here's what you need to know about that: The smaller (more compressed) the file, the faster it will be to send or receive on the Net, but the more likely the compression will be *lossy*, or sacrificing picture quality. Some compression schemes, such as LZW and ZIP for TIFF files, are *lossless*, or nearly so, but they produce bigger files.

As every racing fan knows, there are horses for courses.

Different File Types for Different Purposes

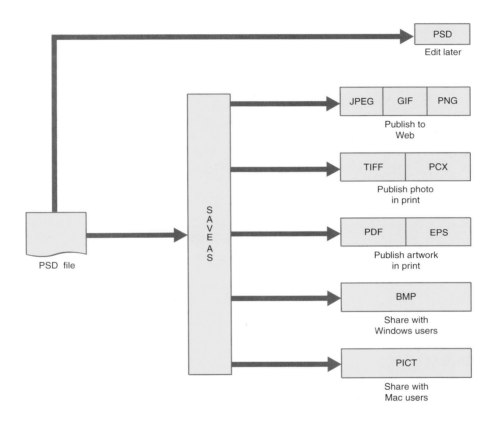

Saving Files in Photoshop Format

Start

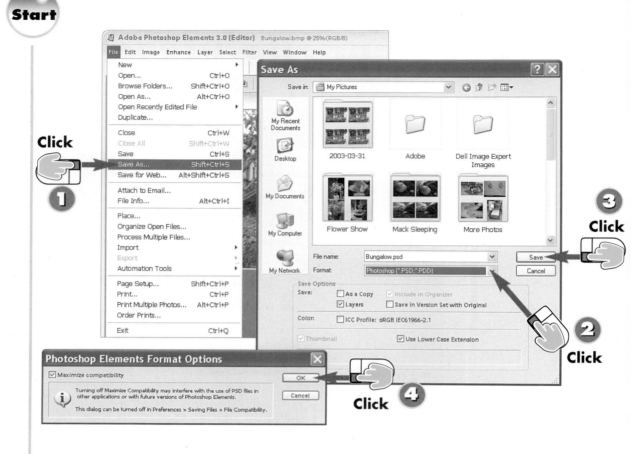

Click

①

③ **Click**

② **Click**

④ **Click**

① With an image open in the active image area, select **File**, **Save As** or press **Shift+Ctrl+S**.

② In the **Format** drop-down menu, select **Photoshop**.

③ Navigate to the location where you want to save the file and click **Save**.

④ Click **OK**.

End

If you've added Elements-specific features to a picture (such as layers, layer styles, shapes, or text), save the file in Photoshop Elements's native format to preserve those features so you can go back and change them later. Even if you're done working on an image, you should save a copy that includes all the layers and other stuff.

Maximize What?

The Format Options dialog box appears only if your picture contains layers. Choosing to save the file for maximum compatibility makes your file larger but ensures that you'll be able to open and edit it in future versions of Photoshop Elements.

Saving Best-Quality Photos for Printing

Start

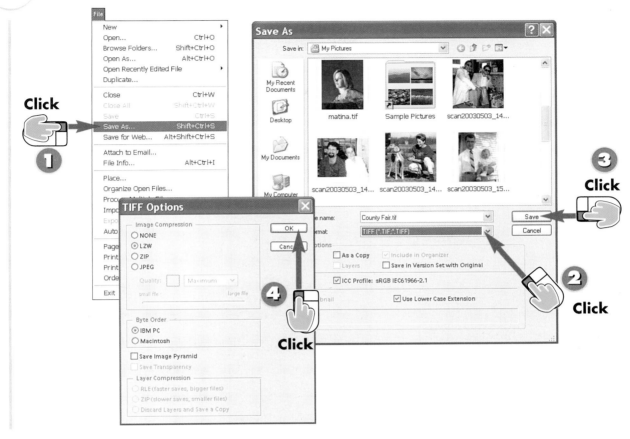

1 With an image open in the active image area, choose **File**, **Save As** or press **Shift+Ctrl+S**.

2 In the Format drop-down menu, select **TIFF**.

3 Click **Save**.

4 Click **OK**.

End

INTRODUCTION

Of all the file formats, Tagged Image File Format (TIFF) is probably the best for saving a high-quality photograph that you intend to submit to a printer or publisher. The result is a file with a **.tif** extension.

TIP

Compression Options
Image Compression: LZW or ZIP are preferable to JPEG. LZW is the safest choice. ZIP can create smaller files, but some users won't be able to open them. Layer Compression: Select **Discard Layers and Save a Copy** unless the recipient needs to edit them.

Saving Designs for Desktop Publishing

Start

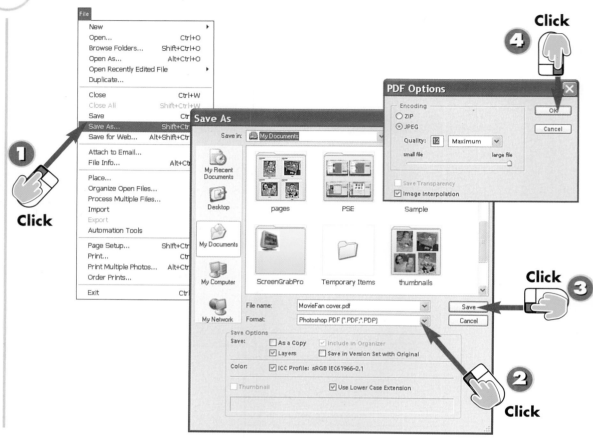

1. With an image open in the active image area, choose **File**, **Save As** or press **Shift+Ctrl+S**.

2. In the **Format** drop-down menu, select **Photoshop PDF**.

3. Click **Save**.

4. Click **OK**.

End

Adobe's Portable Document Format, or PDF, is the best choice for sharing finished-quality images and artwork with anyone anywhere, regardless of the computer make or model they happen to be using. When in doubt about which type of file your recipient can handle, this one is a safe bet.

Encoding Option
In the PDF Options window, even though JPEG is the default value, you'll get better picture quality (but a larger file) by selecting **ZIP** instead.

PSD and Prepress PDF
Although you can convert from other files types when saving, starting with a Photoshop file usually gives the best results. To save as Prepress PDF, which contains print job information as well as image data, upgrade to Photoshop CS.

Saving Files As BMP

Start

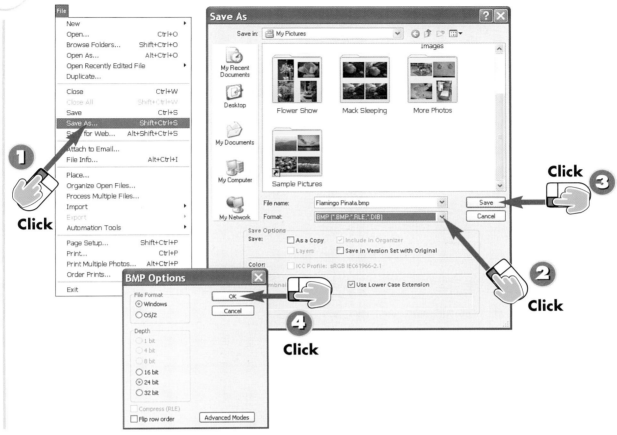

Click ①

Click

Click ③

Click ②

Click ④

① With an image open in the active image area, select **File**, **Save As** or press **Shift+Ctrl+S**.

② In the **Format** drop-down menu, select **BMP**.

③ Navigate to the location where you want to save the file and click **Save**.

④ Click **OK**.

End

BMP stands for bitmap, and it's a common file on Windows PCs for everything from screen captures to files created in paint programs. The filename extension for BMP files is **.bmp**.

Monster Files
BMP files don't use any kind of compression, so they tend to be quite large. If the program or person you're working with can accept PCX format, use that instead. If you must use BMP, you can compress the file after it's saved using a program such as WinZip.

Saving Files As PICT

Click

Click

Click

Click

1. With an image open in the active image area, select **File**, **Save As** or press **Shift+Ctrl+S**.

2. In the **Format** drop-down menu, select **PICT**.

3. Navigate to the location where you want to save the file and click **Save**.

4. Click **OK**.

End

PICT files aren't very common these days because they're a specialized format used only by early versions of the Mac OS. However, for certain purposes (such as creating custom startup screens for old Macs), only PICT will do.

How Many Bits?
The 32 bits/pixel option enables the file to contain more data to describe colors, ensuring that the photo's colors don't change. If file size is a concern, however, choose 16 bits/pixel to save a smaller file.

Applying a Copyright Notice

Start

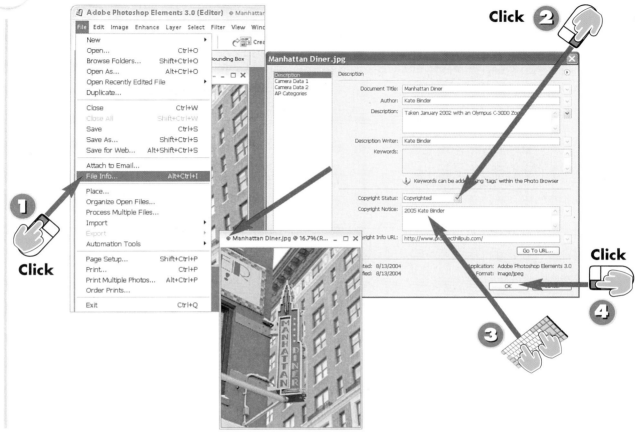

Click ②

Click

Click

①
With the picture in the active image area, choose **File**, **File Info**.

②
Choose **Copyrighted** in the **Copyright Status** drop-down.

③
Type information in the **Document Title**, **Author**, **Description**, **Copyright Notice**, and **Copyright Info URL** fields.

④
Click **OK**. A copyright notice is included in the file information, and the © symbol appears in the image title bar.

End

For copyright purposes, a photographer is considered the author of the image and can hold intellectual property rights (IPR) to it—including licensing its use by others. This task shows you how to append a copyright notice to your images in the form of text data attached to the file.

Getting Permission
If a file you downloaded is marked as copyrighted, the Go to URL button in the File Info dialog box takes you to the author's Web site, where you should find licensing and contact information.

Proprietary Watermarks
Copyrighted images you download from the Web may also contain ownership information as *digital watermarks* in the image itself. To inspect a file for a watermark, choose **Filter**, **Digimarc**, **Read Watermark**.

Saving Files As JPEG 2000

Start

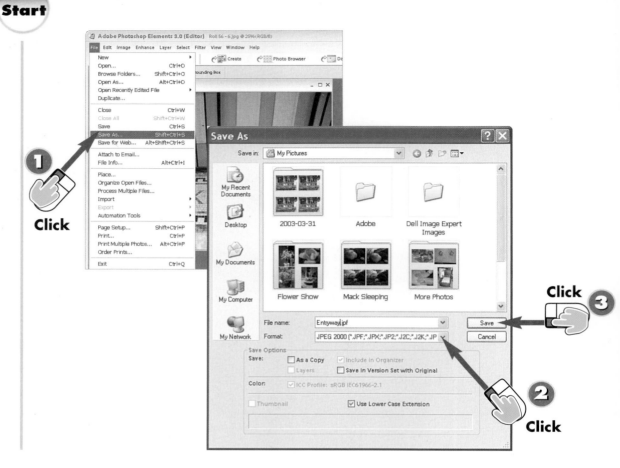

Click ①

Click ③

Click ②

① With an image open in the active image area, select **File**, **Save As** or press **Shift+Ctrl+S**.

② In the **Format** drop-down menu, select **JPEG 2000**.

③ Navigate to the location where you want to save the file and click **Save**.

INTRODUCTION

JPEG 2000 was designed as a new and improved version of the existing JPEG image format. JPEG 2000 files are smaller than JPEG files saved at the same quality level. The ability to save files in JPEG 2000 format is new to Photoshop Elements 3.

What's It For?

Most Web browsers don't yet support JPEG 2000, so it's not a good format option for Web images. But it's a great format to use for archiving and transporting images, particularly large images and pictures with low-contrast edges.

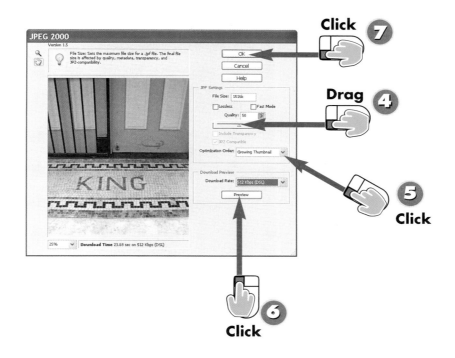

Click 7

Drag 4

Click 5

Click 6

(4) Drag the slider to select a **Quality** level.

(5) Select an **Optimization Order** option, such as **Growing Thumbnail**.

(6) Click **Preview** to see how the image will appear to Web viewers.

(7) Click **OK**.

End

Optimized Viewing
JPEG 2000 offers two new and different optimization options—also known as ways to entertain the viewer while your large images download fully. Growing Thumbnail displays a small thumbnail of the image and then gradually increases the image's size as more data downloads. Color starts out with a full-size grayscale image and then adds color when the color data is received.

Just for Fun

It's only after you've mastered a set of tools that you can begin to take real joy in using them. Then, you can let the logical, step-by-step calculating part of your brain take a back seat and let your imagination do the driving.

If you've worked through most, if not all, of the preceding tasks, you're ready—and you've earned the right—to have some fun. Tasks in this part are all about fooling around, experimenting, and exploring ways of manipulating electronic images like collage artists use paper cutouts and a set of paints.

There isn't space in this little book to take you through all the things you can do with Photoshop Elements. (If, with so many possible choices and combinations, it's even possible.) But with the basic skills you've picked up here, the more your work with this incredibly rich and flexible computer application will seem like play. As you continue to explore, you'll sweat the technical details less and less, and you'll find a marvelous new outlet for your personal expression.

And if, perchance, some of your fantasies seem, er, just a bit bizarre—add a talk bubble or a clever caption and turn them into personalized greeting cards!

Not Quite the Story of My Life

Ever wonder how to turn a simple portrait into a work of art?

Long ago, in a land far away...

Placing Artwork in an Image

Start

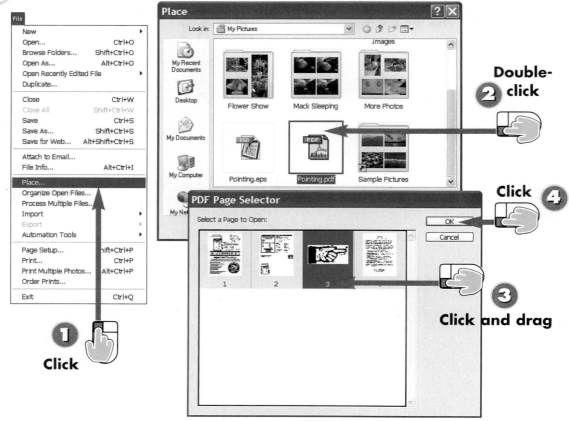

Double-click 2

Click 4

Click and drag 3

Click 1

1 With a background or background image in the active image area, choose **File**, **Place**.

2 Locate and double-click the file that contains the artwork (or select it and click **Place**).

3 If the file contains multiple pages, select the page you want to insert.

4 Click **OK**. The artwork or page is inserted into a new layer in the active image.

INTRODUCTION
Commands you may already have used for combining imagery are File, New From Clipboard; File, Import; and the pair Edit, Copy and Edit, Paste. Here's a handy alternative, a quicker way to insert artwork from an external file that's in one of the other Adobe formats (**.ai**, **.eps**, **.pdf**, or **.pdp** extensions).

Missing Fonts
If you see this warning window after step 3, choose **Continue**, and some other fonts that are available in your computer will be substituted.

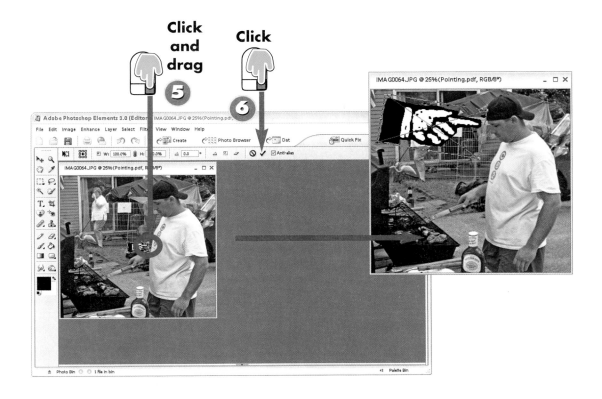

5 Optionally, drag a handle to move or resize the artwork to fit your canvas.

6 Click the **Commit** button, or press **Enter**.

End

PDF Pages and Images
The **File**, **Place** command inserts entire pages from a PDF as new layers. Use **File**, **Import**, **PDF Image** instead to get its images separately. White or background areas in the original become transparent.

Vectors Get Rasterized
Vector graphics in the source file get simplified, or *rasterized* (converted to pixels), when you choose Commit. The objects take on the same resolution as the target image.

Making Mosaic Tiles

Start

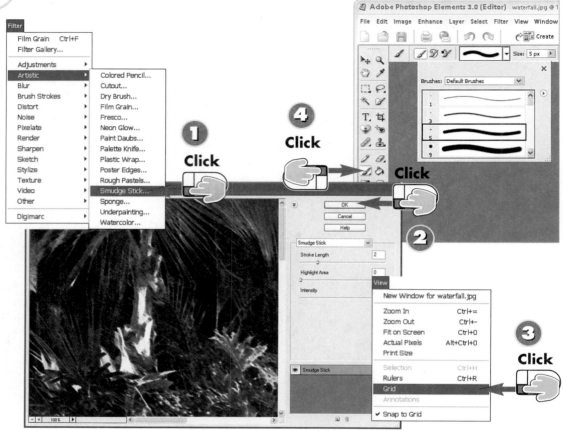

1 Select **Filter**, **Artistic**, **Smudge Stick**.

2 Click **OK**.

3 Select **View**, **Grid**.

4 Select the **Brush** tool and pick a small, soft brush.

Hand-painted tiles are so expensive—and you have to be a real artist to create your own. Unless, that is, you have Photoshop Elements. Here's a quick way to turn any photograph into a pretty convincing tile mosaic.

TIP

Making It Real
Mount your "tiles" on a tabletop using spray adhesive and a few coats of nonyellowing polyurethane varnish. Or put your mosaic on a wall—but mount the paper on a thin sheet of wood first, so you can take it with you when you move.

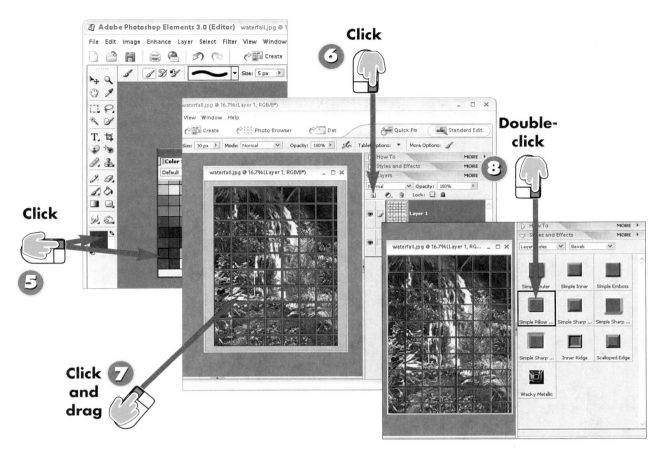

5 In the **Color Swatches** palette, select a foreground color for the grout between the tiles.

6 Click the **Create New Layer** button in the Layers palette.

7 Hold down **Shift** and paint the grout lines along the grid.

8 Double-click the **Simple Pillow Emboss** style in the Styles and Effects palette.

Get Creative!
Try any filter or combination of filters in step 1—you don't have to use Smudge Stick. You can adjust the grout width (select a different brush size) and fiddle with the embossing settings (select **Layer**, **Layer Style**, **Style Settings**).

Changing Your Mind
To change the grout color, make the grout layer active and select a new foreground color. Select **Preserve Transparency** at the top of the Layers palette, and then press **Alt+Delete** to replace all the layer's white pixels with the new color.

Creating Panoramic Views

Start

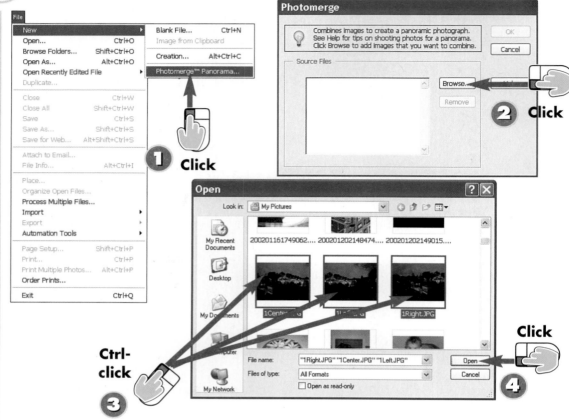

1 Click

2 Click

3 Ctrl-click

4 Click

1 With all files closed, choose **File**, **Photomerge™ Panorama**.

2 Click **Browse**.

3 Ctrl-click two or more images to combine.

4 Click **Open**.

INTRODUCTION

It's truly amazing how sensitive digital cameras are, even in near darkness. These photos were taken in a moonless night, lit only by the glow of city lights. Photoshop Elements has the smarts to blend the edges of several scenic photos seamlessly into one gorgeous panorama.

Pan Your Snaps

HINT

Shots must be adjacent so their edges align: Mount the camera on a tripod. Take your source photos all at the same vertical angle, *panning* from left to right, so that the edges overlap the scene.

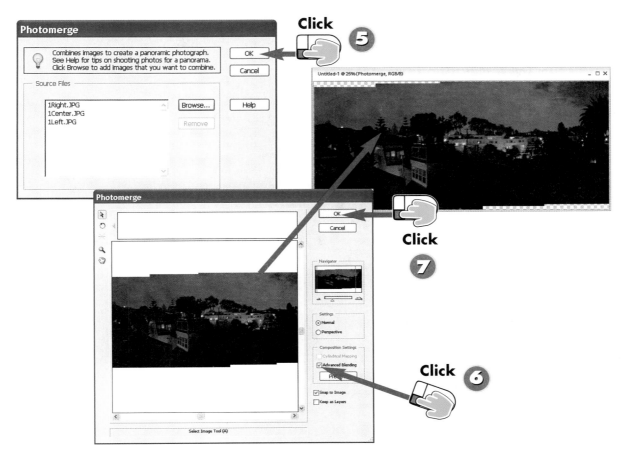

5 Click **OK**.

6 Optionally, check **Advanced Blending** to create seamless edges.

7 Click **OK**. The composite picture appears in the active image window.

End

Photomerge Options
Perspective can heighten the panoramic effect. Available in combination with this option, Cylindrical Mapping emphasizes curvature. Advanced Blending (recommended) not only aligns edges but also makes exposures match.

Crop to Finish
Finish off by cropping the image, because no matter how careful you are, the horizontal edge of the composite image probably won't be smooth.

Achieving a 3D Effect

Start

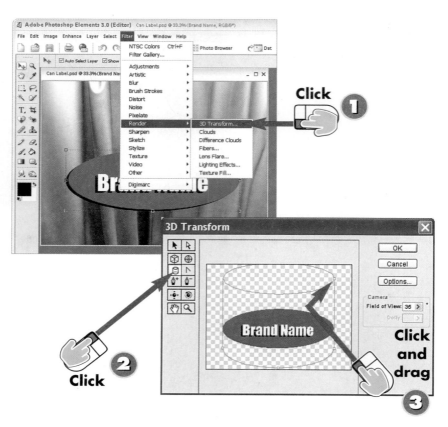

Click ➊

Click ➋

Click and drag ➌

➊ With the object you want to transform selected, choose **Filter**, **Render**, **3D Transform**.

➋ Select a transformation shape, such as **Cylinder** (or press **C**).

➌ Click and drag to size the shape in the 3D Transform preview window.

INTRODUCTION

Three-dimensional transformation opens up all kinds of creative possibilities. Think of the image you start with as being printed on a rubber sheet that you can wrap around a cube, a sphere, or a cylinder.

HINT

Repositioning Vertices
Choose a selection tool; then click and drag any *vertex* (movable point on the shape) to change the outline of the cylinder—to make it look like a vase, for example.

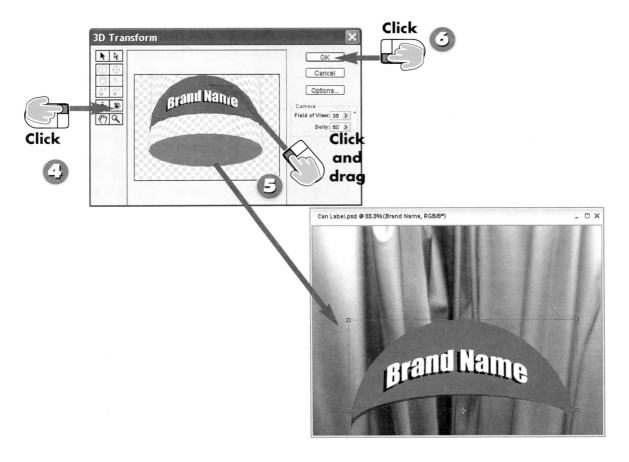

(4) Click the **Trackball** tool (or press **R**). (You can also use the Pan Camera tool or press E.)

(5) Click and drag to adjust the effect in the preview window.

(6) Click **OK**. The transformed object appears in the active image window.

End

Anchor Points
TIP
The *anchor point* is a vertex on the shape to which the image can attach. For the Cylinder shape only, the Convert Anchor Point, Add Anchor Point, and Delete Anchor Point tools become available.

Turning a Photo into a Rubber Stamp

Start

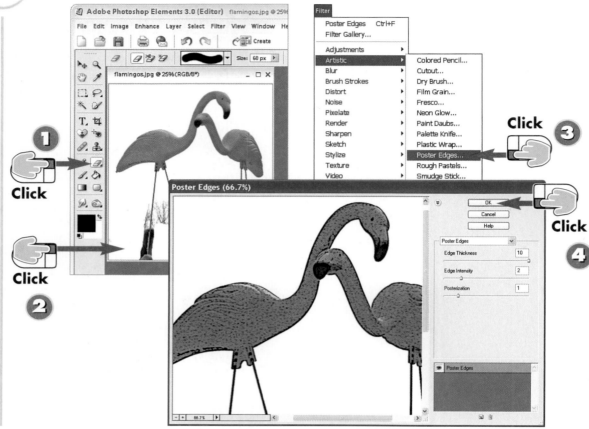

Click ①

Click ②

Click ③

Click ④

① With the image open, select the **Eraser** tool.

② Erase the image's background, leaving only the portion you want to be the stamp.

③ Select **Filter**, **Artistic**, **Poster Edges**.

④ Adjust the settings so the areas that will be the stamp are black; then click **OK**.

TIP

Contrast Is the Key
For best results, choose a picture of an object against a contrasting background. It helps if there's some contrast within the object's outlines, too, unless it's recognizable merely from its silhouette.

HINT

From Concept to Reality
When your artwork is ready, convert it into a rubber stamp by Create a Stamp (**www. createastamp.com**), The Stampin' Place (**www. stampin.com**), Simon's Stamps (**www.simonstamp. com**), or other specialists.

5 Select **Image**, **Mode**, **Grayscale**.

6 Select **Enhance**, **Adjust Lighting**, **Brightness/Contrast**.

7 Drag both sliders all the way to the right and click **OK**.

8 Use the **Eraser** to clean up around the stamp's edges if necessary.

Lighten Up
After step 5, if your picture has a lot of dark gray in areas that you want white, select **Enhance**, **Adjust Lighting**, **Levels** and drag the middle slider to the left to lighten the midtones so they'll drop out to white in step 7.

What Else It's Good For
This technique is also useful for making coloring pages for the kids, t-shirt artwork, or any kind of art that needs to be black on white.

Try Some "Trick" Photography

Start

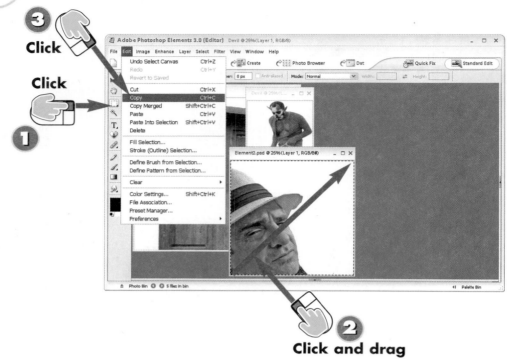

3 Click

Click

1

2 Click and drag

1 Start with three images open—a background and two other images. Click a selection tool, such as **Rectangular Marquee**, or press **M**.

2 Select an object in the first image.

3 Choose **Edit**, **Copy**, or press **Ctrl+C**.

Trick photography takes many forms, but most involve combining and reworking real images to create an unrealistic or improbable scene. This example creates a collage from three separate pictures and then adds some artwork to finish the job.

Managing the Elements

As you combine images, Photoshop Elements inserts them as separate layers. To keep track of layers and control their stacking order, choose **Window**, **Layers** to open the Layers palette.

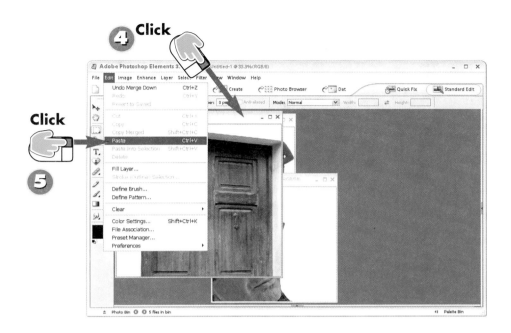

Click (4)

Click (5)

(4) Select the background image by clicking its title bar.

(5) Choose **Edit**, **Paste**, or press **Ctrl+V**. Repeat steps 2–5 to add more objects or images.

See next page

Merry Merging

After choosing **Edit**, **Copy**, a quick way to combine imagery, as shown in some previous tasks, is to use the **Edit**, **Paste Into** command. But remember, when you do this, the insertion does not create a separate layer.

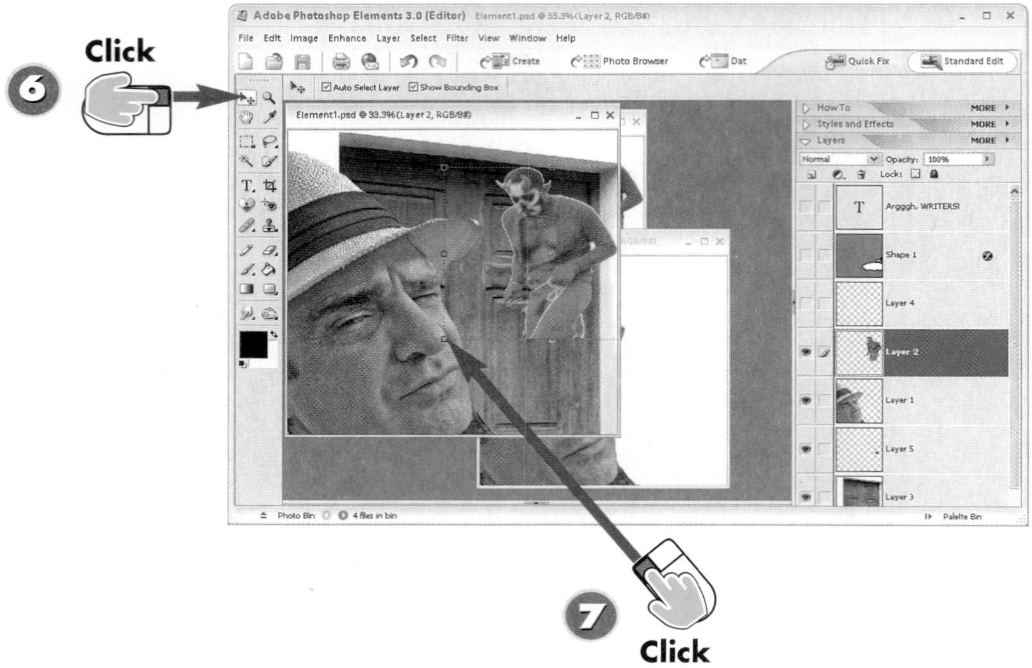

Click

6

7

Click

6 Select the **Move** tool, or press **V**.

7 Click and drag object handles to move or resize the objects and compose the picture.

INTRODUCTION

The ability to combine images in improbable ways apparently brings out the humor in some people. If you use email at all, you've no doubt received pictures of pets doing superhuman feats, celebrities and politicians in compromising positions, or ordinary people with extraordinary physical characteristics!

TIP

Shape Selection

In step 6, if the inserted picture contains multiple shapes, you can use the Shape Selection tool to select and manipulate them individually, as long as you haven't yet simplified or merged the layer.

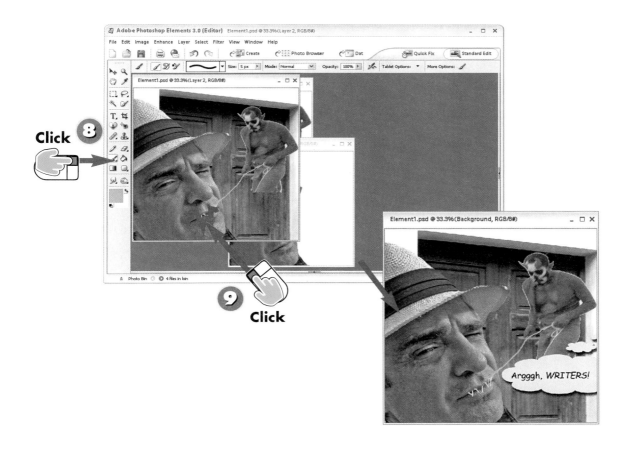

Click 8

9 Click

8 Select a **Brush** tool (or a shape tool).

9 Click and drag to draw on the image. Repeat steps 8 and 9 to add more lines and shapes to your drawing.

End

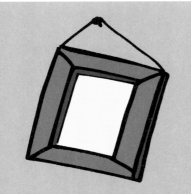

Special Effects
After you've created a collage of images, you can go wild transforming them with any of the commands from the **Image**, **Transform**, or **Filter** menus.

TIP

Getting an Antique Look

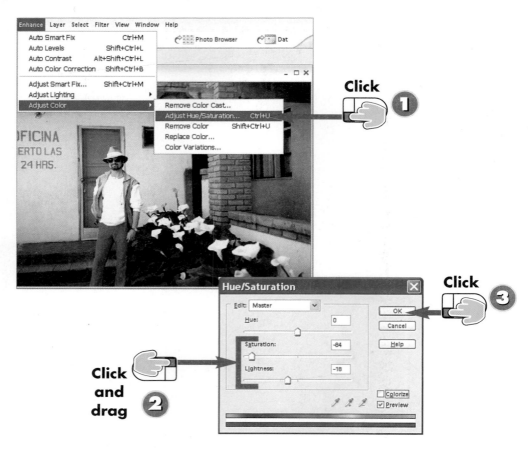

1 With a photo in the active image window, choose **Enhance**, **Adjust Color**, **Adjust Hue/Saturation**.

2 Decrease the **Saturation** and increase the **Lightness** sliders.

3 Click **OK**.

Of course, "antique" is relative to your age—or the ages of the relatives you want to transform. In this case, decreasing the saturation setting creates a look of old, faded Kodachrome. Adding Film Grain enhances the realism, and the Feather effect on the border adds to the impression of a faded snapshot.

Fading and Sepia
Decreasing Saturation can create a monochrome picture, but one that still contains color information. You can then apply Color Variations to get a sepia effect. By contrast, choosing **Image**, **Mode**, **Grayscale** discards all color.

Remove Color Command
An alternative conversion to grayscale that still preserves color information is the command **Enhance**, **Adjust Color**, **Remove Color**, which makes red, green, and blue values equal and reduces Saturation to zero.

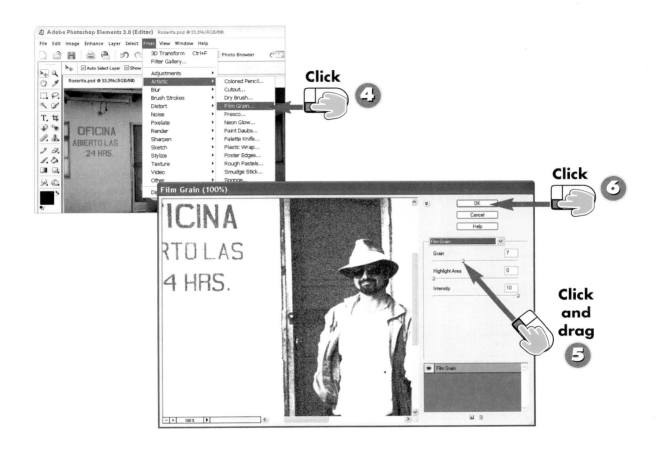

Click 4

Click 6

Click and drag 5

4 Choose **Filter**, **Artistic**, **Film Grain**.

5 Adjust the sliders for effect, such as increasing the **Grain** size.

6 Click **OK**.

See next page

Film Grain
This same type of filter can be applied in the Adobe After Effects application to make your DV movies look like film.

Click 7

Click 9

Click

10

Click and drag 8

7 Select the **Rectangular Marquee** tool, or press **M**.

8 Click and drag to size a border around the picture.

9 Choose **Select**, **Feather**.

10 Click **OK**.

Digital technology has evolved to the point where people are beginning to think its results are too clean and pure to be aesthetically pleasing. For example, it's becoming common practice in music studios to add low levels of audio noise to digital recordings to make them more natural-sounding. As you can see, Photoshop Elements has many ways to make your digital photos funkier and crummier!

Feather Radius

In step 10, remember that the size of the Feather effect is proportional to Image Size in pixels. For example, you may have to increase the Radius value to make the effect more obvious.

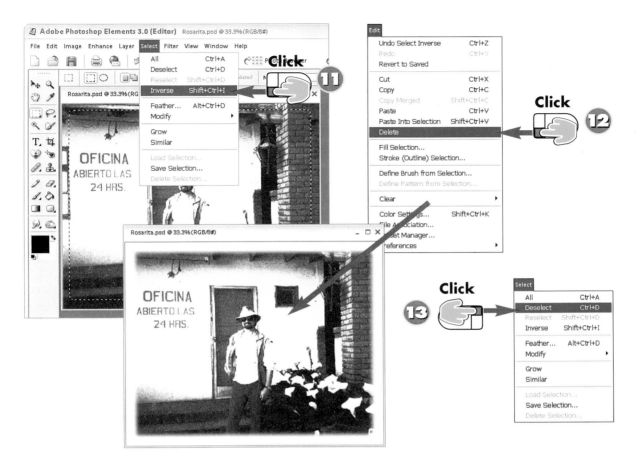

11. Choose **Select**, **Inverse**, or press **Shift+Ctrl+I**.

12. Choose **Edit**, **Delete**.

13. Choose **Select**, **Deselect**, or press **Ctrl+D**.

End

HINT

Experiment!
This kind of experimentation with Photoshop Elements can bring into play any and all of the techniques you've learned in this book. Have fun!

Creating Pop Art

Start

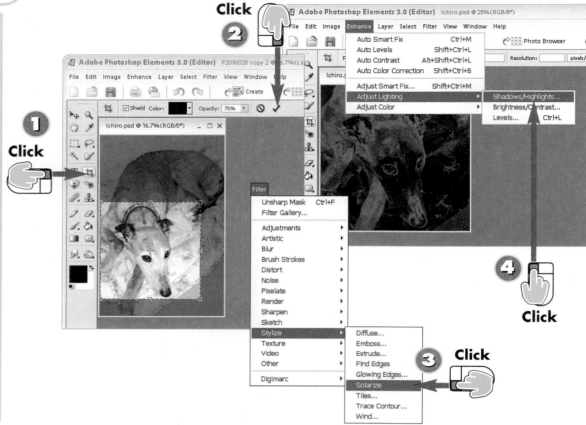

1. Select the **Crop** tool and **Shift-drag** in the image to draw a square cropping marquee.

2. Click the **Commit** button in the options bar.

3. Select **Filter**, **Stylize**, **Solarize**.

4. Select **Enhance**, **Adjust Lighting**, **Shadows/Highlights**.

INTRODUCTION

The biggest advantage of digital photo editing is that you can try dozens, hundreds, or even thousands of variations on a theme for each photo. And putting a few variations together in a collage format just happens to be a recognized art technique, one made famous by none other than Andy Warhol. Give it a try!

HINT

More Options
You don't have to be restricted to different color schemes for your variations. Try applying different Artistic filters. Or line up several copies of an image in a row and make each copy a bit lighter or a bit darker than the one next to it.

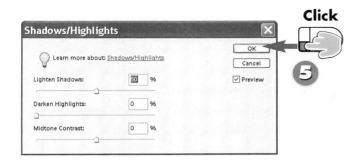

Click

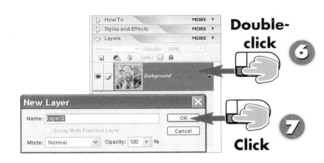

Double-click

Click

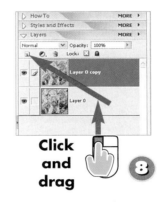

Click and drag

5 Click **OK**.

6 In the Layers palette, double-click the **Background**.

7 Click **OK**.

8 Drag Layer 0 onto the **Create Layer** button to duplicate it.

See next page

Separation of Layers
Putting each copy of the image on its own layer makes moving it around and applying color changes to it easy.

Test Run
Make sure the picture you use has strong enough lines that you'll still be able to tell what it is after you run the Solarize filter. If you're not sure, test it before you spend any time cropping it by selecting **Filter**, **Stylize**, **Solarize**.

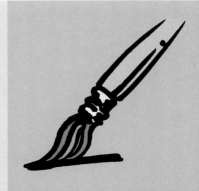

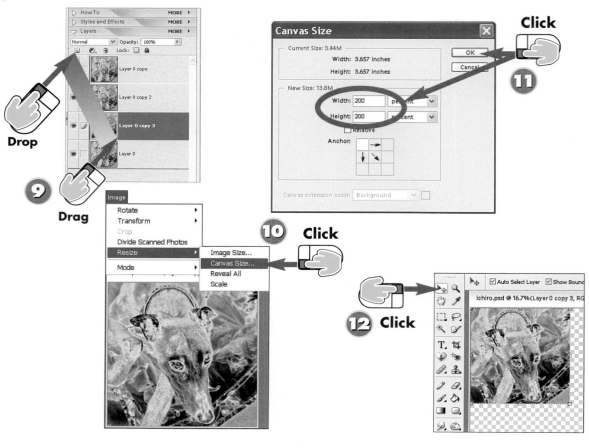

Drop

Drag

Click

Click

Click

⑨ Repeat step 8 twice to create a total of four layers in the image.

⑩ Select **Image**, **Resize**, **Canvas Size**.

⑪ Click the upper-left corner of the proxy grid and set the **Width** and **Height** to 200%; then click **OK**.

⑫ Select the **Move** tool.

Andy Warhol made a similar technique famous with his pictures of Marilyn Monroe, but he also created portraits of other well-known people, such as Jackie Onassis, Che Guevara, and Mao Zedong. Visit the Andy Warhol Museum's Web site (**www.warhol.org**) to see examples of Warhol's work (and to order posters).

A Prerequisite
To select each layer with the Move tool, Auto Select Layer must be checked in the Options bar.

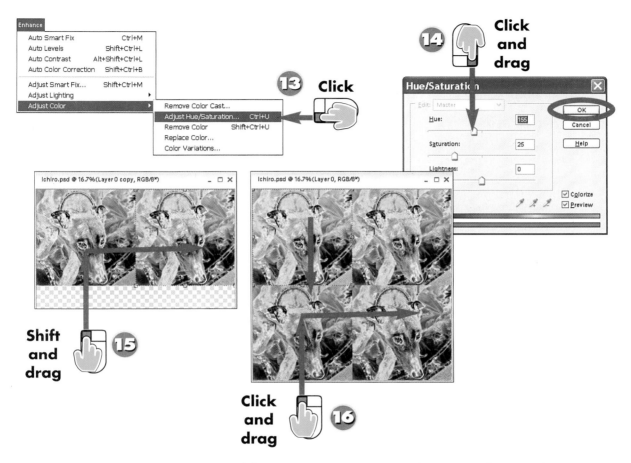

13 Click in the upper-left corner of the image and select **Enhance**, **Adjust Color**, **Adjust Hue/Saturation**.

14 Click **Colorize** and drag the **Hue** slider until you like the image's color; then click **OK**.

15 Shift-drag the picture to the right side of the window.

16 Repeat steps 13–15 to move the other picture duplicates to the bottom corners of the window and colorize them with different colors.

Enlarging Your Color Palette
In step 14, you can adjust the Saturation and Lightness sliders. Leaving these settings the same for all four images provides a more consistent look, but varying them enables you to use a wider range of colors and tints.

Lining Things Up
Press **Shift** as you drag the layers to constrain their movement to 45° angles: straight up and down, left and right, or corner to corner.

Glossary

A

active image area   Application window that displays the image contained in the currently open file.

active layer   Virtual drawing plane, or cel, currently selected in an open image.

adjustment layer   In a multilayered image, a layer inserted to affect the overall appearance of all layers beneath it; in effect, a digital photographic filter.

auto select   Procedure whereby selecting a shape or text object with the Move tool automatically causes its layer to be selected, as well.

autofocus   Automatic focusing capability of digital cameras.

automatic white balance   Digital camera function that sets color rendition on the assumption that the lightest area in the frame is pure white.

B

backlight   Photographic light source emanating from behind the subject.

base layer   When layers are grouped, the bottommost layer that sets the boundaries of the upper ones, determined by the boundaries of a shape on that layer.

bitmap   Digital image composed of pixels; raster image; pixel array; in Photoshop, a black-and-white image.

blending mode   In a multilayered image, a layer option that determines how colors on different layers combine; an option for various tools and filters. Examples: Normal, Dissolve, Hard, Soft.

blow out   To totally overexpose an area of an image so that it is pure white and contains no picture detail.

brush dynamics   Options for the size, shape, and behavior of the Brush tool that control the quality of its brush stroke.

brush tip   Size and shape of the tip of the Brush tool, set in the Options bar after the tool is selected.

burn   In traditional darkroom technique, to underexpose masked areas of a film negative prior to making a print.

C

canvas size   Paper or media size associated with an image file.

caption   Printable text that describes the content of a picture.

capture   To upload image data from a camera, camcorder, or scanner into a computer.

catalog   In Organizer, a collection of image files from which a presentation can be created.

cel   Movie animation artist's transparent sheet of celluloid, analogous to a Photoshop layer.

Clipboard   Scratchpad memory area in Windows through which data, including graphics and images, can be exchanged between open applications.

Close box   X button in the upper-right corner of any Windows window by which it may be closed, or turned off.

collage   Art term for a composition made from cut-out images pasted onto a board.

color cast   Overall tint of a photograph, particularly noticeable and in need of correction when it creates unflattering flesh tones in the subjects.

color components   Separate channels, or primary colors, within a color model; Red, Green, and Blue in the RGB color model; Hue, Saturation, and Lightness in the HSL model.

color management   Coordination of color reproduction devices, such as cameras, computer screens, and printers, so that colors rendered on all of them appear to match.

color matching   Fine-tuning the output of two or more color reproduction devices, such as a screen and a printer, so that colors appear the same on both.

color space   The range of all colors available in a color model.

composite   Combination or merging of two or more images.

composition   Artistic arrangement of subjects within the picture frame.

compression   Mathematical transformation of a digital file so as to describe its contents in fewer bits, thereby creating a smaller file, and degrading its quality or accuracy as little as possible.

constrain   To limit the repositioning or resizing of a shape or text to perpendicular angles; to prevent distortion; to maintain proportions (aspect ratio).

contact sheet   Film photographer's reference print created in the darkroom by exposing filmstrips in direct contact with a sheet of print paper.

contrast   Range of brightness between the highlights and shadows in a photograph.

crop   To reframe an image, moving its edges to exclude unwanted areas.

crushed blacks   Underexposed areas of a picture that are totally black and contain no picture detail.

D

default   Preselected program option settings.

digital watermark   Invisible copyright or proprietary notice within the image area of a photograph that can be read by Photoshop Elements or special reader software; Digimarc.

digitize   To convert a film print or analog video clip to a stream of pixel values; to scan a photo.

discard layers   To merge and simplify all layers in an image at once, rendering text and artwork uneditable as objects; see also *flatten*.

dither   To render a subtle color by juxtaposing dots of two or more primary colors.

dodge   In traditional darkroom technique, to overexpose unmasked areas of a film negative prior to making a print.

dpi   Unit of resolution of a digital printer; dots per inch; equivalent to pixels/inch.

duotone   Two-color image.

DV   Abbreviation of the digital video recording standard.

DVD   Abbreviation for digital versatile disc, optical recording medium for videos and movies.

DVD menu   Onscreen selections of DVD chapters, each indicated by a user-selection button.

E

exposure   Length of time light is permitted to strike a camera's film or sensors (called *CCD chips* in a digital camera).

extension   In a computer filename, characters to the right of the rightmost period, indicating the file type. Examples include **.psd**, **.jpg**, **.doc**, and **.mpeg**.

eyelight   Small photographic light source aimed directly into subject's eyes to make them sparkle.

F

feather   Blurred edges of a shape; vignette.

file type   Indicated by the extension in the filename, a description content data type (such as native Photoshop file) and the associated application required to open it.

fill   Solid area or pattern within a shape, text, or image area.

fill flash   Bright photographic light source used to supplement key light and fill in the area surrounding the subject. In Photoshop Elements, the ability to lighten the darkest (usually foreground) areas of a photo, leaving the bright (usually background) areas unchanged.

filter   In Photoshop Elements, a pre-built artistic effect that can be applied to an image; in conventional photography, a glass covering for a lens that changes the quality of light.

FireWire   Apple trademark for the connection between a camcorder or other device and a computer, designated IEEE 1394; equivalent to Sony's i.LINK.

flatten   To merge and simplify all layers in an image at once; see also *discard layers*.

flip   To create a mirror image of a shape, text, or image.

focus   In Photoshop Elements, to sharpen or blur the edges of a selection; in conventional photography, to adjust the camera lens to achieve the same effect.

folder   In a computer file system, a named directory that contains files.

font   In typography, a typeface in a particular point size; in computer applications, a typeface.

f-stop   Camera setting that controls how much light is admitted during an exposure.

FTP   Abbreviation of File Transfer Protocol, a method of uploading files to the Internet.

G

Gaussian blur   Named for mathematician Carl Friedrich Gauss, a filter that enables finer control over how an image is blurred than does Blur or Blur More.

gradient   Blended color used to fill a shape or background.

grain   Noise filter applied to a digital image to simulate the grain of photographic film.

grayed out   Referring to menu commands or dialog box options that are unavailable based on current settings; dimmed.

grayscale   Monochrome picture that contains shades of black and white.

group   Combination of palettes or layers so they can be manipulated as a single palette or object.

H

halation effect   Artifact of early film that created a beatific glow around closeups of movie stars.

halftone screen   Dot pattern used in commercial printing to render shaded images using tiny, solid dots of black (B&W) or four primary colors (CMYK).

handle   Corner on a selection that can be dragged to resize or reposition the object.

hard   Quality of light that produces sharp edges and dark shadows.

hidden tool   Any tool in the toolbar that can be selected by right-clicking a related tool.

HSL   Color model and mixing scheme based on components Hue (primary color), Saturation (tint), and Lightness (light-dark value).

I–J

ICC   Abbreviation of International Color Consortium, which promotes color standards for the printing industry.

Impressionist brush   Tool used to lay down blurred brush strokes, after the technique of painters who rebelled against doing pictures in painstaking detail.

indexed color   Restricted color tables for specific uses, such as Web or Windows system display.

ink-and-paint   Conventional movie animator's technique of drawing a cartoon character's outline in ink on a clear sheet of celluloid and then filling in solid shapes with acrylic paint.

intellectual property rights (IPR)
Copyrights, patents, and trademarks;
copyright applies to photographs, to
which the photographer is author and
rights holder.

K–L

key light   Main photographic light
source aimed to highlight the subject.

keystoning   Photographic distortion
produced by aiming the camera at a
steep angle, high or low, in relation to
the subject.

landscape   Rectangular image or
printer orientation with the long dimension horizontal.

layer   Separate drawing, painting,
text, or image plane among multiple
planes, or layers, in a Photoshop
image; analogous to movie animator's
cel.

layer style   Options, such as bevels
or drop shadows, that affect all objects
on a given layer.

level   Value of Red, Green, or Blue,
or Black input or output channel to produce brightness and contrast.

linking layers   Marking and associ-
ating layers so that they can be manipulated together.

lossless   File compression that results
in no perceptible loss of quality or accuracy.

lossy   File compression that *does*
result in a loss of quality or accuracy.

LZW   File compression scheme based
on a transformation named for mathe-
maticians Lempel, Ziv, and Welch.

M

mapping   Transformation that bends
and spreads an image or texture over
the surface of an object.

mask   To cover part of an image so
that the area is unaffected by changes
made to other areas of the image.

menu bar   Main pull-down program
selections in an application such as
Photoshop Elements, near the top of the
program window, beginning with the
File menu on the left and proceeding to
the Help menu on the right.

merge   To both simplify and combine
layers in a single operation.

midtone   Pixel values in the middle
range between highlights and shadows.

mixed media   Art term for works
that may combine assemblage, collage,
and painting or drawing.

mode   Image rendering as either
grayscale or color.

monochrome   Single-color image,
but not necessarily black and white.

multisession   Describing a CD or
DVD to which files can be written, or
appended, at different times.

N-O

navigate Procedure for finding files and folders by exploring the file system, based on a hierarchy of files within folders (possibly within folders) on a device (such as a disk).

negative Reverse image from processing camera film, resulting in shadow areas rendered as highlights, highlights as shadows, and color primaries as their opposites (red as green, blue as orange, and so on).

nudge To move a selection by small increments with the Arrow keys.

opacity Degree to which light is blocked by an object or layer; inverse of transparency.

Options bar Settings for a tool, such as Brush, that become available beneath the menu bar after the tool has been selected.

orientation Rotation angle of an image or printout; portrait or landscape.

P

palette Floating window containing effects, commands, and help grouped by category.

palette bin Storage location in the work area for frequently used palettes.

palette tab Handle by which a palette can be selected, docked, or undocked from the palette well.

pan Rotating a camera, typically mounted on a tripod, from left to right or from right to left in the same horizontal plane.

panorama Scenic, wide-angle landscape; Photomerge output.

photo bin Storage location in the work area for currently open images.

picture package Commercial photographer's offered assortment of prints in various sizes, from wallet-sized to larger sizes suitable for framing.

pixel Picture element; colored dot in a bitmap image.

pixels/inch Resolution of a bitmap image; equivalent to printer dots per inch (dpi).

place To insert artwork from an external file into an open image.

plug-in Add-on software module that extends the capability of an application; example: JPEG 2000 filter for Photoshop Elements.

point size Size of type in a selected font.

Pointillize filter Limiting brush strokes to tiny dots of primary color; technique pioneered by Impressionist painter Georges Seurat.

port Input/output channel and connection in a computer.

portrait Rectangular image or printer orientation with the long dimension vertical; headshot.

posterization   Garish color effect produced by the command Image, Adjustments, Posterize.

preferences   User option settings that override default values.

printable area   Rectangular area of a printout that excludes margins by which the printer grips the paper, and therefore where it can't print an image.

profile   Stored color table used for color management.

progressive mode   JPEG file setting that causes a downloaded image to be built up in visible stages, intended to improve the viewing experience over slow connections.

publish   Upload files to the World Wide Web.

R

rasterize   To convert a vector shape or type object to pixels; to simplify.

recipe   Sequential instructions delivered by the Help system for performing a specific task.

red eye   Undesirable reflection in a subject's eyes caused by flash photography.

redo   Reverse the previous Undo command.

related topics   Help selections that appear in the Hints palette after doing a search.

render   To apply changes to a digital image and display or print it.

resample   To change the resolution (pixels/inch) of an image.

reset   To return to previous option settings.

resolution   Measure of picture quality or degree of detail; pixels/inch; dpi.

retouch   To use artistic techniques to improve the appearance of photographic subjects or scenes; in portrait work, to soften wrinkles, remove blemishes, and so on.

revert   To cancel pending edits without saving and return to the original version of a file; see also **undo**.

RGB   Color model and mixing scheme used in Photoshop Elements, based on components Red, Green, and Blue.

S

search field   Text box in the upper-right center of the Photoshop Elements work area into which a text description of a problem or task can be typed to trigger searching of Help files.

selection   Active object or area within the image area to which the next command or operation will be applied.

sepia   Tinted monochrome image; typical of antique photographs.

shape   Geometric object in Photoshop Elements; examples: Rectangle, Ellipse.

sharpen   To increase pixel contrast at object boundaries; to bring into focus.

shortcuts bar Row of buttons with icons just beneath the menu bar, representing single-click activation of commonly used commands.

simplify To convert vector shape or type to pixels; to rasterize.

skew To apply a spatial transformation to a selected object that causes its sides to be slanted.

slider Program control in some dialog boxes, toolbars, and palettes that can be adjusted by clicking and dragging.

soft Blurred; out of focus.

stacking order Priority of layers in a multilayered image that determines visibility of objects; objects on upper layers will obscure overlapping objects beneath.

still Single-frame photographic image (as opposed to moving image created by a sequence of frames in a movie or video).

streaming video Video clip, usually low resolution, optimized for downloading over the Web.

superimpose To overlay one graphic object on another.

swatch A single, saved color; one of a table of color selections coordinated for a specific purpose, such as Web-safe colors.

system colors Set of swatches containing only colors displayable without dithering on Windows computers.

T

texture Variegated surface or area; pattern.

thumbnail Small, low-resolution image used to preview file selections without incurring the delay of opening the full-resolution file.

title bar Top band on any Windows window showing the name of its selections (or filename of the image or document it contains), and by which the window may be moved by clicking and dragging.

tool Selection, drawing, and retouching tools found in the Photoshop Elements toolbar, located by default on the left edge of the work area.

toolbox Collection of Photoshop Elements tools, located by default on the left edge of the work area.

ToolTip Name or function of a tool or button, as well as its shortcut key (if any), which pops up when you hover the pointer over it prior to making a selection.

transparency Degree to which objects and colors on underlying layers are visible; the inverse of opacity.

tutorial Online training lesson available through the Help menu.

type mask   Type-shaped selection area, typically used to create hollow text to let the background or lower layer show through.

U–V

undo   To reverse or cancel the most recently executed command or change; see also **redo**.

undock   To open a palette from the palette well; see also **dock**.

ungroup   To make a previously grouped set of palettes or layers accessible individually; see also **group**.

upload   To transfer a digital file from a device, such as a camera, camcorder, or scanner, to a computer; to capture.

USB   Abbreviation for Universal Serial Bus; a type of computer port that supports digital cameras and printers.

vector   Mathematical description of a geometric object; a resolution-independent object description.

vignette   Portrait with feathered edges.

W–Z

Web site index page   Home page on the World Wide Web.

WIA   Abbreviation of Windows Image Acquisition, a standard for connecting scanners and cameras to computers.

work area   The Photoshop Elements desktop display.

ZIP   Lossless file compression scheme.

zoom   To magnify the view of an image.

Index

Numbers

How can we make this index more useful? Email us at indexes@quepublishing.com

H

halftone images
    previewing, 174-175
    radius, 174
    resolution, 174
haliation effects, 140
Healing Brush tool, 136
help, finding, 19
hiding layers, 161, 163
hollow text, creating, 90-91
Horizontal Type tool, 77
hue, antique effects, 212-215

I

image area
    adjusting, 8-9
    viewing, 8-9
image sizes, controlling, 183
images. *See also* **photos; pictures**
    Acrobat images, importing, 38
    adding to artwork, 198
    adjusting with sliders, 49
    antique effects, 212-215
    archiving on CDs, 44-45
    backgrounds, mounting, 98-100
    black-and-white, modifying, 104-106
    blurring, 112
    borders, adding, 60-61, 94-96
    brightness/contrast, modifying, 66
    color, adjusting, 50
    color cast, correcting, 63
    colors, 64-67, 70-71
    cropping, 50, 52, 203
    customizing, 208-210
    drawing, 116
    edges, softening, 69
    feathering, 214
    fixing, 172-173
    formatting, undoing, 51
    gradient fills, creating, 97
    halftone images, 174-175
    importing from cameras, 24
    layers, 164

    lighting, adjusting, 50
    merging, 209
    naming, 25
    negatives, scanning, 37
    optimizing, 35
    optimizing for the Web, 182-183
    organizing, 6
    painting, 116
    panoramic views, creating, 203
    perspective, transforming, 58-59
    posterizing, 108
    preparing for the Web, 181-182
    printing, 39, 75
    printing picture packages, 42
    quick fixing, 48
    red-eye, removing, 62
    resampling, 56, 60
    resizing, 39, 56
    retouching, 130-131
    rotating, 54-55
    saving, reverting to last, 51
    scanning, 26-27
    sending via email, 180
    shapes, creating, 118
    sharpening, 68
    sharpness, adjusting, 50
    sizing, 94
    sizing to fit page, 75
    skies, replacing, 102-103
    slides, scanning, 34-36
    slideshows, creating, 153
    still images, capturing, 178-179
    straightening, 53
    text, adding, 72-75
    text, editing, 77
    text, modifying fonts, 78
    text, overlaying, 76
    video, capturing from, 30-31
    video, copying from Clipboard, 32
    video, copying from Web pages, 33
    video, grabbing from, 28-29
importing
    images, 26-33, 37
    images (Acrobat), 38
    images from cameras, 24
    images from slides, 34-36
Impressionist Brush tool, 11, 127

How can we make this index more useful? Email us at indexes@quepublishing.com

T

Tagged Image File Format (TIFF), 189

talk bubbles, adding, 87

Temperature slider, 49

text
- adding, 72-75
- alignment options, 76
- deleting, 79
- distorting, 83
- drop shadows, adding, 89
- editing, 77
- effects, applying, 88
- flipping, 82
- fonts, editing, 78
- growing, 83
- hollow, creating, 90-91
- moving, 79
- overlaying, 76
- printing, 74-75
- resizing, 80
- rotating, 82
- selecting, 77
- skewing, 83
- talk bubbles, adding, 86-87
- transforming, 83
- vertical, creating, 81
- warping, 84-85

text alignment options, 81

text lines, adding, 81

text properties, 78

textures
- backgrounds, 100
- glass, 113
- oil paintings, 106-107
- sketch effect, 109

TIFF (Tagged Image File Format), 189

Tint slider, 49

titles
- adding, 72-73
- slides, adding, 155

toning tools, 131

toolbox, 10-11

tools, 10-11
- Crop, 52
- drawing, 116
- Horizontal Type, 77
- Lasso, 70-71
- Move, 79
- painting, 116
- Rectangular Marquee, 98, 100
- Red Eye Removal, 62
- settings,changing, 12-13
- Vertical Type, 81

transforming
- 3D effects, 204-205
- images, antique effects, 212-215
- perspective, 58-59
- text, 83

trick photography effects, applying, 208-210

trimming
- contours, 142
- photos, 114

troubleshooting, 18
- slides, 36

tutorials, 19

type mask, 90

U-V

undoing
- Eraser tool, 126
- formatting, 51

uploading
- images from cameras, 24
- Web pages, 148

VCD, 150

vector graphics, rasterizing, 199

vector shapes, modifying, 160

vertical text lines
- adding, 81
- options, 81

Vertical Type tool, 81

vertices, positioning, 204

Rather than having you read through a lot of text, Easy lets you learn visually. Users are introduced to topics of technology, hardware, software, and computersin a friendly, yet motivating, manner.

Easy Digital Cameras
Mark Edward Soper
ISBN: 0-7897-3077-4
$19.99 USA/$28.99 CAN

Easy Creating CDs & DVDs
Tom Bunzel
ISBN: 0-7897-2972-5
$19.99 USA/$30.99 CAN

Easy Windows® XP, Home Edition
Second Edition
Shelley O'Hara
ISBN: 0-7897-3036-7
$19.99 USA/$30.99 CAN

Easy Digital Home Movies
Jake Ludington
ISBN: 0-7897-3114-2
$19.99 USA/$28.99 CAN

Special offer!

Save 25% on Easy Digital Cameras

Easy Digital Cameras is the perfect book to help you learn to take pristine pictures using all the features of your digital camera. Then it shows you how to edit them for perfection and share them with your friends and family (whether you print them, burn them to a CD, or share them online via email or the Web).

Purchasers of *Easy Photoshop Elements 3* get two chapters from *Easy Digital Cameras* on this CD, and a special discount of 25% off the purchase of *Easy Digital Cameras*! To get your discount, go to www.quepublishing.com, look up *Easy Digital Cameras*, and enter discount code ESYCAM when prompted at checkout, and you will get a 25% discount and free shipping! Take advantage of this special offer today.

Offer expires January 15, 2005.

License Agreement